Great Exhibits!

Great Exhibits!

An Exhibit Planning and Construction Handbook for Small Museums

Beth Hansen

ROWMAN & LITTLEFIELD
Lanham • Boulder • New York • London

Published by Rowman & Littlefield
A wholly owned subsidiary of The Rowman & Littlefield Publishing Group, Inc.
4501 Forbes Boulevard, Suite 200, Lanham, Maryland 20706
www.rowman.com

Unit A, Whitacre Mews, 26-34 Stannary Street, London SE11 4AB

British Library Cataloguing in Publication Information Available

Library of Congress Cataloging-in-Publication Data Available

978-1-4422-7075-6 (cloth)
978-1-4422-7076-3 (paper)
978-1-4422-7077-0 (electronic)

♾™ The paper used in this publication meets the minimum requirements of American National Standard for Information Sciences—Permanence of Paper for Printed Library Materials, ANSI/NISO Z39.48-1992.

Printed in the United States of America

Contents

Please go to https://bethsagehansen.wordpress.com for helpful links and supplier information.

Photos and Table

Table

Preface

The majority of museums in the United States are small, or very small. The volunteers and staff at these museums want to present the best exhibitions possible. Yet books about developing exhibitions are aimed at large museums with full staff in many departments. These books give instructions such as "have your preparator mount the artifacts" and "your graphic designer will have suggestions for the appropriate font." What is a person at a small museum to do?

Small museums can have exhibits as dynamic and interesting as large ones. With just a few volunteers and a little money, any group of volunteers and staff can create professional-quality exhibits. They just need to know how to do it.

The basic process for creating an exhibition is the same for any museum of any size. Someone needs to do the work of the educator, curator, designer, and so forth. What makes small and large museums different are the number of people and the amount of money available. Volunteers and staff at small museums need to learn to be "jacks of all trades" and make things work on a shoestring budget.

Museum Studies students can benefit from learning to think like small museum staff. By taking the viewpoints of various personnel, they will be better team members in a museum of any size.

Great Exhibits! will guide the reader through the entire process of creating exhibitions—from developing ideas to writing labels to installing artifacts. It will ask the reader to think about issues such as visitor studies and artifact care. In other words, it covers every topic a book for a large museum would cover, but it assumes the museum has fewer people to do the work and less money to spend.

The genesis of this book came from years of working with community groups and small museums. As a curator with an MA in Museum Studies, I was often the only professionally trained staff person at any small museum in the county, or in a three-county area. I worked with other nearby museums on their collections management projects, as well as exhibits. I helped a group of people start a new museum and create their first exhibition. I am pleased to report that the volunteers there are still going strong. Mostly, I created exhibitions for my museum with the help of the local community. The best exhibitions were focused on small neighborhoods and villages and were created entirely by a volunteer team from that area. I led them through the exhibition development process as they decided how to lay out the room, which stories to tell, what color to paint the walls, and which artifacts to loan the museum for the exhibition. This process was tried and tested numerous times. If the steps outlined here are followed, the museum will end up with a professional-quality exhibition.

Use in Small Museums

Great Exhibits! is intended to help small museums improve their exhibitions without breaking their banks. It assumes that they may have only one staff member and a crew of volunteers with no professional museum training. The most difficult part of this book for a small museum will be finding out it exists—so please help by spreading the word about this resource.

Naturally, I hope the volunteers and staff at small museums will read the chapters in order and make good use of the worksheets in each one. They were written from years of experience, and will save museum staff hours of work caused by having to go back and do things a second time.

This book was written in a style I hope will be readable and engaging to encourage museum volunteers or staff members to actually read it all. I know that people who work in small museums already have much to do and little time to spare. So this book is pared down to the essentials that you really need to know to create a professional-looking exhibition.

Use in Museum Studies Courses

On the other end of the spectrum, Museum Studies has professionalized museum work. A generation ago, such programs were rare, and museum staff had to learn on the job. Today's museum professional has earned a master's degree and knows much about the theories of how to meet accreditation standards.

Numbers alone tell us that many graduates of these programs do, or will, work in small or very small museums. The Institute of Museum and Library Services (IMLS) estimates that there are thirty-five thousand museums in the United States, and almost seventeen thousand of them are historical societies, which tend to be small, local museums. According to the American Alliance of Museums (AAM), 57 percent of their members work at museums with a staff size of zero to three. There are many, many more small museums that IMLS and AAM don't know about.

Great Exhibits! was designed to be academic enough to meet the standards of any graduate-level museum studies program. As an adjunct faculty member in Museum Studies, I am aware of the requirements for such course work, and this book is based on the curriculum developed for graduate students. The text outlines the duties of each staff person, while realizing that one person may carry out all of them. Although it is written in a casual tone, it is academically sound.

It is recommended that the chapters be read in order, as many build on each other. Faculty are encouraged to use the worksheets as the basis for papers on each chapter. In my class, I ask students to write reports to the museum director outlining the exhibition committee's work, utilizing the questions on the worksheet.

This paragraph is for Museum Studies faculty who need to justify the use of this textbook: staff in all positions at a museum can become involved in developing exhibits. It is important to know the theories and reasons behind good development in order to become a productive member of the team. Expertise is required from educators, collections managers, and administrators, as well as curators or other content experts. *Great Exhibits!* will provide an introduction to the process of creating exhibits and prepare students to be a productive member of an exhibit development team. Author Beth Hansen has an MA in Museum Studies from John F. Kennedy University, has worked in museums for over twenty years, and teaches Exhibition Development as adjunct faculty.

For Everyone

Museum professionals know that there are many aspects to consider when creating a museum exhibition. A look at the contents will show that this book covers the entire process from concept to installation. The sources used are some of the best researchers and practitioners in the field. While no specific topic is covered in depth, every topic is covered. Readers who want to know more about any specialized area can check the sources listed in the bibliography. In its way this book is like the volunteers and staff at a small museum—they have to know about a wide variety of subjects but don't have to be experts at any of them.

The chapters in this book are written in the order they should be read and carried out. The first six guide the reader through the "thinking" process of making decisions about the exhibition topic and content. The last chapter provides instructions for the "doing" process of building exhibit cases and mounting objects. Up-to-date resources and supplier lists are found on the website.

Museum professionals need to start by thinking about the nature of exhibitions (chapter 1) and then who they have available to create the exhibition, and when it can be done (chapter 2). Selecting the specific topic is the next task (chapter 3). Collection volunteers and staff then research the collection and decide what can be exhibited, and if anything needs to be borrowed. Hands-on activities will be considered, as well as room colors (chapter 4). Label writing is so important that an entire chapter is devoted solely to that process (chapter 5). The exhibition team then will learn about the importance of evaluation, and how to test a mock-up (chapter 6). Finally, comprehensive instructions are provided on how to physically build the exhibition (chapter 7).

By the end of the book, readers will be knowledgeable about every aspect of creating an exhibition for a small museum. They will know how to consider the visitors' perspectives, care for artifacts in the museum's collection, and effectively communicate a concept through exhibition. These skills will all be carried out at the lowest cost possible, as every topic in this book requires more time than money.

The Website

Information about suppliers and links for helpful websites are constantly changing, so they are on the website rather than in print. Please consider the website a vital part of this book. Go to rowman.com, then find the book to access current information.

Just as a great exhibition depends on visitor feedback, so a book about exhibits depends on reader feedback. Please access the website to share your experiences with other readers and to provide corrections and updates.

Acknowledgments

As with any book, there are many people who helped make this project possible.

Thomas Anovick read my instructions and drawings to tell me if they made sense, and took photos when I needed help. He was also there in many other ways, offering support throughout.

Kathy Quackenbush proofread and edited all the chapters for me. You have her to thank if this book is readable.

Beverly Serrell is my personal goddess of the art of label writing. Her book has inspired me for years, and she was kind enough to read my chapter on labels.

Friends and family read various parts of this to give me feedback on their areas of expertise. I am especially grateful to Eric Heath who provided great input on the instructions and drawings.

John F. Kennedy University's Museum Studies program gave me my professional start. I thank the university for admitting me to the program and introducing me to the women who taught me Exhibition Development—Darcie Fohrman and Lisa Mackinney.

I learned a great deal at every museum I worked, and from every professional staff person I worked with. Thank you to the Indian Cultural Museum at Yosemite National Park, San Pablo Historical Society, Los Altos Historical Society, Hayward Area Historical Society, Oakland Museum of California, and the Historical Society of Talbot County. Special thanks to the museum directors who taught me exhibition skills: Jim DeMersman, Glenn Uminowicz, and to Yosemite curator Craig Bates.

Small museums like the ones I have worked at would be nothing without their volunteers, so thank you to all the volunteers who worked on exhibitions at museums with me, and who handled other areas of museum work while I was busy with exhibits.

Arminta Neal, author of *Help for the Small Museum* and *Exhibits for the Small Museum*, inspired my hands-on exhibition skills. This book started out as an attempt to update hers.

Certainly not least, and perhaps most, I would like to thank Mom and Dad for helping to finance college. I hope I've made you proud.

Chapter 1

Why Create an Exhibition?

Congratulations to you for reading this page. The majority of people who pick up this book will flip directly to one of the pages on how to construct exhibit furniture. But some of you are reading this first chapter, and you will get insights that the others will miss.

If you are reading this in preparation to open an exhibition in a few days, you will be greatly disappointed. Museum exhibitions require planning. There are some steps in this book that you will have to do only once, such as making a model of your exhibition space and buying equipment. But most of the actions will have to be repeated each time you think about a new exhibition. I recommend you give yourself at least three months to work on an exhibition.

I'm going to stop here for a brief definition: an exhibit is one element, such as a single case or panel, while an exhibition is the entire display of many cases and panels.

Statistically, most very small museums are history museums. Historical societies and history museums make up 55 percent of all museums in the United States, according to the Institute of Museum and Library Services (IMLS.gov, 2014), but I realize that there are small museums on every topic under the sun.

Why Do Museums Create Exhibitions?

Why do museums create exhibitions? There are a few basic reasons:

- To display the objects the museum owns

- To get people to come to the museum

- To carry out the museum's mission to preserve and educate

A successful exhibition will combine all of the reasons above, as well as encourage people to support your organization with their time, concern, and money.

Museum exhibitions can do something nothing else in the world can—show people the real things. Anyone can take a virtual tour of the world's great museums on the Internet. But people still go to museums. Why? "We have the real things," wrote Kathleen McLean, a museum exhibition consultant. "It is the interactions among people, real objects, phenomena, and ideas that make museum exhibitions unique. Exhibitions are the essence of a museum experience" (McLean, 1993: 15). Likewise, Teresa Goforth wrote in *Small Museum Toolkit 5*,

> Museum exhibits tell stories in the most compelling and fascinating way. They pull people to them through sights and sounds and the promise of "the real thing." They provide visual context to a multitude of rich stories that, without the work of small museums all over the country, might not otherwise be told. (Goforth, 2012: 49)

Museum's Mission

Your museum has a mission statement that summarizes why it exists. If you don't know what it is, go find it. Way back when the museum was founded, someone put it on the forms sent to the IRS to get the 501(c) 3 nonprofit status. That form should still be in a filing cabinet somewhere.

The mission statement probably reads something like "to preserve ———— and to educate the public about ————." Every exhibition you produce should fit into that mission statement. If you are a rock and mineral museum, it doesn't make much sense for you to spend your resources creating an exhibition on hand-painted fans of the eighteenth century. No one will think to come to your museum to see that exhibition, and people who come to see rocks will be very disappointed. It certainly doesn't carry out your mission statement.

Yet not following the mission is one of the most common mistakes that museums make. I've done it—many organizations have done it. Usually we've been talked into it by someone who has a collection they want to display or a point they want to make. We take on the exhibition because we hope it will help generate goodwill. I have to say, it rarely does.

Learning from Experience: An influential person at the history museum had heard about an exhibition of produce crate labels that was available to rent. This person was adamant that we should bring it to our history museum. The museum was in an area that had once been agricultural, and the art was historic, so eventually we gave in. We got the delivery of the identical black frames holding the produce labels and hung them on the wall. The next week, I got yelled at (actually yelled at) by a group of ladies who had brought their friends and were disappointed to find just flat, two-dimensional artworks on the walls. "You usually have such good exhibits of interesting things!" she fumed at me. Word got around, and the museum stayed mostly empty for the eight weeks we had that exhibition. History buffs didn't have a lot of interest in an exhibition of art prints, and art aficionados didn't think to come to the history museum.

Permanent or Temporary?

If you are lucky, your museum has enough space to accommodate both a permanent and a temporary exhibition. But even if you only have one exhibition room, you need to consider this concept. These types of exhibitions serve different purposes and different audiences. You will need to decide which you want to create before you go any further in this process.

Permanent

The permanent exhibition will always be there for new visitors and for people bringing their friends for the first time. It explains the basics of the topic your museum covers.

A great example of the permanent exhibition is the visitors' center at any state or national park. The visitors' center is your first stop because there you will get an overview of the park. There will be maps, photos, or dioramas on the flora and fauna, a history of the site, and information about what to do in the park.

This permanent exhibition should be easily accessible from the front entrance so that first-time visitors will be able to find it. In an ideal situation, there is also a way to bypass it so that visitors who have already seen it can go straight to the temporary exhibition.

As you can imagine, your museum will be willing to spend more time and money on an exhibition that will be on display for years than on one that will only be up for a few weeks or months. You may want to permanently mount light fixtures and make other changes to your space to enhance the exhibition's appearance.

Temporary

Temporary exhibitions allow you to delve deeper into some aspect of your museum's mission. The museum can rotate the objects on display and bring items out of storage. It encourages visitors who have already been to the museum to come back and see something new.

Here are some ideas for temporary exhibition topics:

- An important person or place. It is the perfect way to celebrate the anniversary of an event.

- One type of artifact—hats, model train cabooses, meteorites, teacups.

- Seasonal topics. These can include "Back to School" in the fall and "Vacation" exhibitions full of postcards and family photos in the summer. In a rural area, exhibitions can change according to the tasks being done in the community. In a community that welcomes tourists, the tourist season exhibition can be a general interest topic, and the off-season exhibition can focus on an issue that only locals would be concerned with.

- Current events. Is your community debating new zoning ordinances? The museum can explain how the old ones were determined. Is the hospital considering moving to another town? Highlight the history of the organization. Are mute swans competing with native tundra swans? Tell people about the situation.

Now the time has come for you to take action. Your assignment is to fill out Exhibit Worksheet 1: Exhibit Basics. Who else do you need to involve in this decision? Who else cares what the public sees in the museum? Do you need to get the board to approve the budget? The next chapter will discuss the people you will want to round up to help you develop the exhibition.

Worksheet 1

EXHIBIT WORKSHEET 1: EXHIBIT BASICS

OUR MUSEUM'S MISSION STATEMENT: _____

_____

_____

_____

_____

TEMPORARY OR PERMANENT: _____

IF PERMANENT, EXPLAIN WHY: _____

_____

PROPOSED LOCATION: _____

EXHIBIT PLANNING & PREPARATION TIME: _____

PROPOSED OPENING DATE: _____

PROPOSED CLOSING DATE: _____

PROPOSED BUDGET: _____

To-Do List

Set up a meeting with a few people to help you decide on a topic.

Fill out Worksheet 1: Exhibit Basics.

Sources

Goforth, Teresa. "The Truth, the Whole Truth, and Nothing But the Truth: Researching Historical Exhibits." In *Small Museum Toolkit 5, Interpretation: Education, Programs, and Exhibits*. Edited by Cinnamon Catlin-Legutko and Stacy Klingler, 49–70. New York: Rowman & Littlefield, 2012.

Institute of Museum and Library Services. "Government Doubles Official Estimate: There Are 35,000 Active Museums in the U.S." IMLS.gov press release dated Monday, May 19, 2014.

McLean, Kathleen. *Planning for People in Museum Exhibitions*. Washington, DC: Association of Science-Technology Centers, 1993.

Chapter 2
Who Will Create the Exhibition and When?

Before you get too far into thinking about your exhibition, you need to consider who will work on it and how much time it will take. If this is your first exhibition, you may be surprised at the amount of time you will need to successfully complete all the steps. But by carefully planning what will happen and when, you will save yourself heartache and sleepless nights.

Who Will Create the Exhibition?

You may have already answered the question, "Who will create the exhibition?" with the statement "I will." Hopefully, you are lucky enough to have a few people to help you with various aspects. As you go through the list of tasks, you may realize that you have volunteers whose skills will be useful in one area or another. People are often more willing to promise to volunteer for a few hours than for an entire project.

Large museums have committees of staff members who work on exhibitions, but I know you don't. Even if you are the entire committee (and I have been), it is helpful to remember to look at the project through the eyes of the various professionals who would be on a large committee. Therefore, we'll look at what some of those roles are before we move on to talk about how you can organize your exhibition development project.

Curator magazine featured an article by Janet Kamien in which she laid out four key roles:

Content specialist (curator, researcher)

It's the responsibility of this role to provide the content and assure the accuracy of that content. . . . Which objects and archival materials will best support the content and be of interest to visitors?

Designer

The designer's primary task is to provide the three-dimensional frame for the exhibit's elements. . . . How will the exhibit be made most visually engaging? What props, environments, or devices might be conceived to support content and engage visitors?

Content interpreter (developer, interpretive planner, educator)

The utility of this role is predicated on the notion that a scholar or researcher view of the content is usually not the same as the visitor view, and must be edited and translated for the visitor to best understand and appreciate. . . . What organization and selection of material, ideas and experiences will make this exhibit content most accessible to its largest audiences?

Project manager

This is the nuts and bolts role of oversight of schedule and budget. . . . How should the process of creating this exhibit be organized? (Kamien, 2001: 120)

I know what you are probably thinking—I don't have people to do all of those jobs! Remember, many volunteers are willing to help with a small aspect of a project. Do you have someone who is a teacher? Someone with a great sense of color and design? Anyone who is handy with a hammer? You may be lucky enough to be able to put together a committee.

When you think about people who can help you, keep in mind that they need to work well together. The Smithsonian Institution published a guideline for its staff and pointed out, "The team approach stresses roles and process. The team needs to establish shared goals and objectives for the exhibition, share and balance authority and responsibility for a project's vision and outcome, and reach agreement by consensus" (SI.gov, 2002).

Still can't come up with people to fill these roles? Well, then you can do all of them, or as many of them as you need to. You won't have to put in more hours; you will just need to remember to think from different viewpoints now and then.

People who work at small museums are used to wearing more than one job "hat." When they go to conferences they attend the educators' breakfast, the collections managers' lunch, and the directors' cocktail hour.

You will learn how to think from various viewpoints. Personally, I have stood in the collection storage and had arguments with myself about whether an object should be in an exhibition.

Education self: "This artifact would be perfect. It is a great example."

Collections Management self: "But it is fragile. It defeats the museum's purpose of preserving artifacts if I ruin it by putting it on display."

Curatorial self: "Maybe I can rotate it on and off of exhibit and use an inferior example some of the time."

If you are not already having these types of conversations, you will be soon, as you become a museum staff unto yourself.

Here are some suggested functions for you and/or your exhibition team:

- Project Management: oversee progress of the exhibition

- Curatorial: research the "content" or subject matter of the exhibition

- Collections Management: take care of the objects

- Education: plan programs and make sure the visitors understand the exhibition

- Design: create the layout and look of the exhibition

- Installation: build the actual exhibition

- Marketing/Publicity: let the public know about the exhibition

- Museum Store: select items to sell in the museum store as souvenirs

Now that you have some idea of what the various jobs involve, you can make a copy of Exhibit Worksheet 2: Exhibit Team, and fill it out for your own project.

Worksheet 2

EXHIBIT WORKSHEET 2: EXHIBIT TEAM

COMMITTEE MEMBERS AND THEIR SKILLS:

Role	Person's name	Special Skills s/he brings to the job
Project Management	_____	_____
Curatorial	_____	_____
Collections Management	_____	_____
Education	_____	_____
Design	_____	_____
Installation	_____	_____
Marketing/Publicity	_____	_____
Museum Store	_____	_____

OUTSIDE VOLUNTEERS/VENDORS:

_____

_____

_____

_____

_____

Timeline

Perhaps it is human nature to wait until the last minute to meet a deadline. So you will create a timeline for the project because the work necessary to create an exhibition simply cannot be done the day before it opens. This will give everyone deadlines for their areas of responsibility.

The sample timeline below assumes you are starting from the very beginning and includes many details, but don't let it scare you.

SAMPLE EXHIBIT TIMELINE

Task	Due Date	Responsible Role(s)
Finalize Topic Selection	March 1	Exhibit Committee
Seek Objects/Photos to Display	April 1	Curatorial and Collection Management
Initial Room Layout Plan	May 1	Design
Finish Research	May 30	Curatorial
Propose Programs	May 30	Education
Write Press Releases	June 30	Marketing/Publicity
Build Exhibit Furniture	June 30	Installation Team
Test One Component	July 1–15	Curatorial and Education
Order Store Merchandise	July 1	Store Management
Write Labels	July 1	Curatorial and Education
Paint Exhibit Furniture	July 15	Installation Team
Paint Walls	July 30	Installation Team
Install Objects & Labels	August 10	Collection Management and Design
Install Labels	August 15	Curatorial, Design, Education
Set Lights	August 17	Installation Team
Set Up for Opening Party	August 19	Exhibit Committee

Now you can create your own timetable in Exhibit Worksheet 3: Timeline. Fill in your tasks and dates and the names of people on your team (even if most of the names are your own). I recommend starting at the bottom with the opening date and working your way backward up the chart.

Worksheet 3

EXHIBIT WORKSHEET 3: TIMELINE

Task	Due Date	Responsible Role(s)/Person(s)
_____	_____	_____
_____	_____	_____
_____	_____	_____
_____	_____	_____
_____	_____	_____
_____	_____	_____
_____	_____	_____
_____	_____	_____
_____	_____	_____
_____	_____	_____
_____	_____	_____
_____	_____	_____
_____	_____	_____
_____	_____	_____
_____	_____	_____

Who Will Create the Exhibition and When?

At the conclusion of this chapter, you have now completed the groundwork for your exhibition. You have an idea of the topic, what work needs to be done, who will do it, and when it will be completed. Congratulations—you have finished the most boring part. From now on it gets more fun.

To-Do List

Call some volunteers.

Fill out Exhibit Worksheet 2: Exhibit Team.

Fill out Exhibit Worksheet 3: Timeline.

Check the additional resources on our website.

Sources

Kamien, Janet. "An Advocate for Everything: Exploring Exhibit Development Models." *Curator* 44, no. 1 (2001): 114–28.

Smithsonian Institution. "The Making of Exhibitions: Purpose, Structure, Roles and Process." Washington, DC: Smithsonian Institution, Office of Policy and Analysis, 2002.

Chapter 3

What Will the Exhibition Be About?

Topic and audience are intertwined. Your audience may help determine your topic, or your topic may determine your audience. For example, if most of your visitors are fourth-grade students on field trips, you will want to install an exhibition that they can understand and that engages them. On the other hand, if you want to do an exhibition on steam engines, your target audience will be mechanics and engineers, if you can think of how to get them to come.

But getting people to see your museum exhibition is not as simple as "build it and they will come." There are lots of museum employees and volunteers who can tell you sad stories of great exhibitions that were seen by very few people.

So it is worth your while to spend a little time figuring out who currently comes to your museum and what they want to see. Then you will have a better idea of which topic to exhibit.

Audience

Why Visitors Come

Why do people go to museums in general? As much as museums would like to think that visitors come to learn interesting facts, social reasons are much more important. In the 1990s, John H. Falk and Lynn D. Dierking shook up the museum world by determining that visitors see museums as a leisure-time activity. They conducted extensive visitor surveys and found that museums are competing with the ball game, the shopping mall, and the park. Most people go to museums in a group, often a multigenerational family group. Their ongoing research since then has only confirmed this finding (Falk and Dierking, 2013: 41). A visit to your museum probably started with a discussion a few weeks before the day of the visit. These are the main questions people ask themselves when considering going to a museum:

- How much time will it take?

- Is it easy to find and is parking available?

- How much will it cost?

- Is the environment pleasant?

- Is it a good place to go with family and friends?

- Will the children enjoy it?

- Will we learn something or enjoy seeing things?

- Will we have fun? (Falk and Dierking, 2013: 43)

Notice how far down the list the word *learn* occurs. Yes, you want your exhibition to be accurate and educational, but the museum needs to be pleasant and enjoyable.

Who Are Your Visitors?

Who comes to your museum? Who do you wish would come to your museum? You have to answer both of these questions before you can start to design your exhibition.

Chances are, most of your current visitors are tourists. It is an interesting fact that people go to museums when they are on vacation but not when they are at home. Try this informal experiment: ask your friends and family if they've ever been to the museum in their hometown. Odds are, most of them will say they've always intended to get to their local museum someday. If they actually went to the museum, it was probably because someone from out of town was visiting. Even the Smithsonian Museums find that only 15 percent of their visitors are local (Smithsonian Institution, 2004).

We do know a few basic facts about museum visitors in general. An early scholar of museum audiences was C. G. Screven. He worked in the psychology department of the University of Wisconsin and brought his psychology background to the study of museum audiences as early as the 1980s. In 1986, he wrote in *Curator* magazine:

Most visitors have a number of things in common:

1. Better education and higher socioeconomic levels than the general population.

2. Social or family orientation. Most visitors come in small groups of two or three.

3. Visual orientation. Primary interest is toward visual exploration of the exhibition environment—mainly objects or other dramatic elements. . . . Low priority visuals include passive two-dimensional wall panels and traditional text. (Screven, 1986: 110)

Almost thirty years later, Beverly Serrell wrote a very similar description: "Museum visitors are a diverse group of fairly well-educated, mostly middle-class people seeking a culturally oriented, leisure social outing" (Serrell, 2015: 49).

How can you find out who your museum visitors are? Just ask them. As you welcome visitors and chat with them, ask them if they live nearby or are visiting the town, what else they are doing that day, and so forth.

Keep a log book at your front desk with attendance records. This can be as simple as putting a few headings across a page in a notebook. You can even ask local people for contact information so you can get them on your newsletter list.

Date

Number of people in party

Adults

Children

Hometown

Email

This information will be very important when you fill out grant applications. Almost any funding agency wants to know how many people visit your museum. Kathleen McLean wrote that "visitor surveys are useful for identifying the museum audience—who the visitors are and where they come from. . . . This information is a valuable long-range planning tool" (McLean, 1993: 71).

Target Audience

It's tempting to say, "Our exhibition will appeal to everyone." But the reality is that this is a very difficult goal to achieve. You are better off to pick a target audience for your exhibition. You will be much more successful at pleasing some of the people all of the time than trying to please all of the people all of the time (to paraphrase Abraham Lincoln).

Museum Studies professor Duncan Grewcock recommends that you have an idea of your intended audience and what they already know about the topic, and what they want to see and do in the museum (Grewcock, 2014: 35).

As noted above, most visitors are tourists. There is nothing wrong with targeting that audience and trying to get as many of them to see your museum as possible. What else do you know about them? Do you tend to get tourists with children? Or are most of your visitors retirees? How much time do they want to spend in the museum?

Naturally, you hope that your exhibition will attract new local people who will love the museum, become members, volunteer their time, and donate lots of money. Can you be more specific about which people you want? Schoolchildren? Newcomers? Natives? Retirees? Parents?

The good news is that every exhibition will bring in some people who have never been to your museum before. If you provide them with a quality experience, they will be likely to come back to your next exhibition. As Barry Lord said, "The visitor should have a good time, and in the course of that pleasurable experience should begin to discover a new, broadened interest or valuation of the subject matter of the exhibition" (Lord and Piacente, 2014: 13).

Topic

What will the exhibition be about? Hopefully you've already decided if you are building a permanent or temporary exhibition. If you haven't, go back to chapter 1.

You may want to pick a topic that someone at your museum knows about, or you may want to do research for the exhibition. Hopefully, you found someone (and perhaps that is you) to perform the curatorial tasks as you were forming your committee in the last chapter. If you didn't read the job descriptions, go back to chapter 2.

Museums have a great honor and responsibility—we are among the most trusted institutions in the country. Small museum curator Teresa Goforth titled her article on exhibitions "The Truth, the Whole Truth, and Nothing But the Truth: Researching Historical Exhibits." In it, she wrote:

> Museums have a responsibility and an obligation to present only the most accurate and current information to their audiences. Visitors trust museums to provide them with "the truth," insofar as that is possible, and all museums must honor that responsibility. To do so requires a passion to dig for clues and piece together the facts that make up the stories that combine to create the fabric of our communities. (Goforth, 2012: 49)

If the person handling the curator tasks doesn't have a topic in mind, you can look to your membership for ideas. Member surveys are one way to solicit ideas (you can read about that later in this chapter). Sometimes your members will offer great suggestions, but other times your committee will have to say "thank you, but no thank you." Eugene Dillenburg and Janice Klein explain why a committee provides an excellent way to deal with these situations:

> Since exhibition ideas can come from a variety of sources both inside and outside the museum, one way to ensure the broadest possible input is to create a mechanism for the ongoing or periodic compiling of exhibition ideas. This can range from an exhibition suggestion box to regular community meetings. It is also important to have a formal review system in place to make sure the appropriate criteria are met and to provide a way of saying no. Formal approval of exhibition topics by the director or a board committee is one way to ensure this. (Dillenburg and Klein, 2012: 72)

Types of Exhibitions

A few basic types of exhibitions are: object based, topic based, phenomena demonstration, and people based (McLean, 1993: 22).

Object Based

You may have an interesting collection of objects in your museum's storage. These may, or may not, make for a compelling exhibition. Have you somehow ended up with a variety of duck decoys, teapots, or needlepoint samplers? Most history museums have wedding dresses and have done an exhibition on weddings through the years. Your object-based exhibition is more likely to gain a wide audience if various people have donated the items. Each person who has something they donated on exhibit will come to see it. They will probably come back with friends to show them.

Sometimes museums will mount a temporary exhibition showing the new donations. These are a great way to let the public know they will see something they have never seen before and for donors to feel proud of what they have contributed. But be aware that whatever you display, at least five other people will tell you they have one or two, and will offer to give you theirs. Be prepared to add some delightful loans or donations while the exhibition is open (or to tactfully reject them—you can blame it on the committee).

Learning from Experience: A museum had a variety of items from local businesses—matchbooks, piggy banks, paper weights, and so on. These were attractive objects on their own, and many local people remembered shopping at those stores, which made the exhibition a fun experience for locals.

It also had a collection of buttons. Hundreds of buttons were sewn onto black velvet and mounted into frames. While a costume specialist might really have enjoyed looking at the details of various buttons, the rows of frames of little round buttons were not especially appealing to the general public. The exhibition was remembered, but not in a good way—there was a joke about it in the local newspaper ten years later, when a columnist sarcastically said a new event was so exciting the museum should revive the button exhibit to celebrate.

Topic Based

Many towns have some good stories in their pasts. You need a story that spans some time and involves multiple people. What happened after the freeway bypassed the town? Or when the schools were desegregated? What did downtown look like before the mall was built? Were people laid off when a manufacturing facility was closed? Or did prosperity come to town with a new industry?

Just remember that your story, like a river, can be either deep or wide. You can tell one story really well in this exhibition and get deep into that subject. Or, you can cover a big topic, such as the town history, and just tell the basic facts. You can only fit so much in your exhibition space or in your visitors' heads. All the other good stuff can go in the accompanying booklet or website (more on that later).

Phenomena Demonstration

Many science and natural science museums attempt to demonstrate scientific principles. History museums can, too. How does a corn shucker work? How do you spin wool? What does a butter churn do to make milk into butter?

Put out working objects that are not part of your collection and let people play with them. You can buy replicas or nearly worn-out objects just for this purpose. They will be part of your education collection. For an exhibition on the development of technology in the home, I bought a nonelectric vacuum cleaner and set it out for people to play with. (It worked by pumping a handle to create suction.) After the exhibition was over, the vacuum went back on eBay.

People Based

Sometimes exhibitions are about people, or a person. If you are involved in your hometown museum, the first thought that probably crossed your mind was your own family story. I'm sure your ancestors are just as fascinating as mine, but an exhibition about your glorious ancestors probably won't attract many visitors and new members. You wouldn't want to travel to my town to see an exhibition about my ancestors. Sorry, but other people probably feel the same way about yours, unless your ancestor includes George Washington, in which case you can ignore everything I just said.

The museum is better served by creating an exhibition about the people who lived in town at a certain time or worked in a certain field. Then you can feature everyone's ancestors by making sure you have photos of as many people as possible. In fact, put a story in your newsletter and the local newspaper telling people what you are looking for. The children and grandchildren of those people will be only too happy to let you scan their family photos. It is important to offer to scan them so people can keep their treasured originals.

Member Survey

An important question in considering an exhibition is: Will anyone want to see it? Does it matter if you mount the world's best exhibition on the life cycle of the sea slug if no one comes to view it? I'm sure there are sea slug fans out there and I don't want to insult them, but you can see that it is probably not a popular topic among the general public. You want to bring visitors into your museum so they can see the value of your organization.

One way to determine if the topic will draw crowds is to do a survey. Don't panic—this will be easier than you think. There are survey websites available for free on the Internet, and you can send a link in an email. Or you can include a printed survey in your newsletter. Make sure it is a separate piece of paper that folds over to display your preprinted return address on the back. When creating a survey, I usually include one topic that is either very silly or a real dud just to make sure people are actually reading the form.

A survey is a good way to weed out subjects that you just don't think will work without offending the people who suggested them. "Well I thought sea slugs was a great topic," you can say, "but our member survey indicated that people just weren't very interested."

Sample Survey

Our museum is considering the installation of temporary exhibitions over the next couple of years. Please indicate which topics would interest you, with 1 being the least interesting and 5 being the most.

The First Cars in our Town	1	2	3	4	5
Lifecycle of the Bumble Bee	1	2	3	4	5
Copper Mining and Miners	1	2	3	4	5
History of Socks	1	2	3	4	5
Stores Downtown in 1950	1	2	3	4	5
Hats through the Centuries	1	2	3	4	5

Suggest your own exhibition topic: _____

Develop the Topic

Now that you've picked a topic that visitors will want to see and designated a curator/expert, you get to start planning the actual exhibition. (You thought I'd never get around to this point, did you?)

First you need to define the big idea. Tell me in one or two sentences what your exhibition is about. If you can't describe it in that few words, your story is too big. You need to narrow it down. Museum exhibition expert Beverly Serrell wrote that the big idea "is the first thing the team, together, should write for an exhibition. A big idea is big because it has fundamental meaningfulness that is important to human nature. It is not trivial" (Serrell, 2015: 7).

Create an outline of your exhibition story. Each Roman numeral should be a section of the exhibition, comparable to a chapter in a book. Your exhibition doesn't have to be large. Each section can be just one panel or one exhibit case. Just make sure you have enough content to fill out the exhibition.

Sample Exhibition Story Outline

Topic: The Story of Our Town

I.   Native Americans
II.   Colonists/Settlers
III.   Village Becomes a Town/City
IV.   Major Industry(ies)
V.   Twentieth-Century Utilities (phones, sewers, street lights, etc.)
VI.   Post–World War II suburbs
VII.   Our Future

Public Programming

Another way to get people into your museum is by offering public programs. Programs are a whole separate topic in the world of museums, so I will only touch on it here. I mention it at all because an interesting program can attract someone who has never visited, or encourage someone who has seen the exhibition to come back to your museum.

Did you find someone for your committee who can handle the educational tasks for this exhibition? I know, it may be you, again. So put on your educator hat and think about this for a few minutes.

A wide variety of activities can be offered as public programs. The most common is a lecture. Someone knowledgeable on the subject can give a lecture. There are benefits to having your own local curator talk about the topic, and different benefits to bringing in a new face from outside of your area. Your Humanities Council probably has a list of speakers who will come to your museum for little cost.

Arts and crafts activities are very popular, too. The most common kind is called "make it and take it" in which people get to create a finished item during one workshop. If the exhibition is on lace, a lace-making class is an obvious fit. But you can go a little farther out from the main topic. For example, an exhibition that featured historic correspondence inspired a class in calligraphy. It was so popular the students asked for it to become a series of classes.

It's OK to charge a fee for a program. The amount people are willing to pay depends upon the perceived value of the class. Look around your community and see what other organizations are charging for art classes, lectures, and other activities. In the case of an outside lecturer or instructor, find out how much they want to get paid and add on a few dollars for the museum. Naturally you can charge more for an appearance by a person who is already well known and doesn't often talk in your area.

Collaboration with other organizations or businesses in your community will often result in a rich variety of programming, with less work on your part and perhaps twice the audience.

- Your library is an obvious choice—they probably have books on just about any topic and may know authors who want to come talk about their books.

- An exhibition on pottery led to a collaboration with a paint-your-own pottery studio, in which photos of the pieces on exhibit were laid out at the studio for inspiration.

- The local archaeology club may be able to help you organize your collection of arrowheads and give a wonderful set of lectures.

- A film festival worked with a museum to select independent films that fit with the museum's exhibition and showed them at a local auditorium as a fundraiser for both organizations.

I know I keep going on about having a committee to help you. But this is another time when you might be able to get people to just attend a couple of meetings to select program topics. They may know people who can give talks. Most of all, having other people to run ideas past will help you reach the best decisions.

There are entire books and websites about how to develop museum programming. I hope you will encourage your education volunteer to spend a little time getting inspired by them.

This chapter has given you a lot to think about and do. Take your time on this—it is terribly important. Once you have a good, solid topic that you know people are interested in and that you can provide information about, you are on the road to creating a successful exhibition.

Worksheet 4

EXHIBIT WORKSHEET 4: EXHIBIT TOPIC

OUR MUSEUM'S MISSION STATEMENT: _____

_____

_____

TARGET AUDIENCE FOR THIS EXHIBIT: _____

_____

STATE THE TOPIC IN ONE SENTENCE: _____

_____

REASON WE THINK IT WILL BE POPULAR: _____

_____

WRITE THE OUTLINE OF THE EXHIBIT ON THE BACK OF THIS WORKSHEET

ORGANIZATIONS WE CAN COLLABORATE WITH: _____

_____

IDEAS FOR PUBLIC PROGRAMS WE CAN OFFER WITH THIS EXHIBIT:

(IDEALLY ONE PER MONTH)

_____

_____

_____

_____

_____

What Will the Exhibition Be About?

To-Do List

Conduct a survey of possible exhibition topics.

Start a visitor log, if you don't already have one.

Fill out Exhibit Worksheet 4: Exhibit Topic.

Check the additional resources on our website.

Sources

Dillenburg, Eugene, and Janice Klein. "Creating Exhibits: From Planning to Building." In *Small Museum Toolkit 5, Interpretation: Education, Programs, and Exhibits*. Edited by Cinnamon Catlin-Legutko and Stacy Klingler, 71–97. New York: Rowman & Littlefield, 2012.

Falk, John H., and Lynn D. Dierking. *The Museum Experience Revisited*. Walnut Creek, CA: Left Coast Press, 2013.

Goforth, Teresa. "The Truth, the Whole Truth, and Nothing But the Truth: Researching Historical Exhibits." In *Small Museum Toolkit 5, Interpretation: Education, Programs, and Exhibits*. Edited by Cinnamon Catlin-Legutko and Stacy Klingler, 49–70. New York: Rowman & Littlefield, 2012.

Grewcock, Duncan. "Before, During, and After: Front-End, Formative, and Summative Evaluation." In *Manual of Museum Exhibitions Second Edition*. Edited by Barry Lord and Maria Piacente, 33–39. New York: Rowman & Littlefield, 2014.

Lord, Barry, and Maria Piacente. *Manual of Museum Exhibitions, Second Edition*. New York: Rowman & Littlefield, 2014.

McLean, Kathleen. *Planning for People in Museums Exhibitions*. Washington, DC: Association of Science and Technology Centers, 1993.

Screven, C. G. "Exhibitions and Information Centers: Some Principles and Approaches." *Curator* 29, no. 2 (1986): 109–37.

Serrell, Beverly. *Making Exhibit Labels: A Step-by-Step Guide*. Nashville, TN: American Association for State and Local History, 1983.

Serrell, Beverly. *Exhibit Labels: An Interpretive Approach*, Second Edition. New York: Rowman & Littlefield, 2015.

Smithsonian Institution. *2004 Smithsonian-Wide Survey of Museum Visitor's*. Smithsonian Institution Office of Policy and Analysis, Washington, DC. Accessed 2016. https://www.si.edu/content/opanda/docs/Rpts2004/04.10.Visitors2004.Final.pdf.

Chapter 4

What Will People See?

Now you get to start thinking about what the exhibition will look like. This gets fun. What objects and photos will be displayed? What sort of atmosphere and feel will the exhibition convey to your visitors? Will it be light-hearted? Serious? Cheery? Brooding?

If you have been lucky enough to build a committee, this phase can use input from everyone. If you are working alone, you can try to look at the project from a variety of viewpoints.

Objects and Photographs

What objects and photos will help tell the story of this exhibition? This is the section for the volunteers who are taking on the tasks of curation and collections management. Or, if you are the solo exhibition developer, it's time to put on the curation/collection management hat. You get to play in the collection. (In the most careful, professional manner possible, of course. But it's still fun.)

You want to highlight your museum's collection, but you are not limited by it. You can borrow or buy anything you want to add to the exhibition. We'll talk more about that later.

If you find that you just don't have enough objects and photos, you may want to rethink the exhibition topic. Perhaps you need to tell another story.

On the other hand, if the exhibition is timely or important, you may have to get creative. During the War of 1812 bicentennial, museums in states involved in the battles frantically called each other, desperate to borrow objects from the era to display. It turned out that nobody had very much—there are only about three uniforms still in existence. It was an important event to mark, though, so everyone made do. Even the Naval Academy at Annapolis had to create an exhibition almost entirely composed of paintings of battles—most of them created decades after the events. Local history museums developed exhibitions of life at home during the War of 1812 because they had furniture, lamps, and clothing, or told stories of local battles illustrated by maps.

Research Your Collection

What does your museum have in its collection that relates to this particular exhibition story? This is why collection volunteers have spent hours recording donations, cataloguing photographs, and organizing storage. Just like in a library, your collection is only useful if you know what you have and where things are.

For now, we are going to assume that you know what you have, but if you need help with cataloguing your collection there are many excellent books and websites out there that can take you step by step through the process. Also, there are some wonderful software programs available for relatively little money.

Cast a wide net for items that may add detail to your exhibition. Subjects to search can include:

- Specific topic of your exhibition

- The time period

- The names of any people involved

- Places where events happened or types of places (such as marshes)

- Specific items (such as tools)

Borrow or Buy

Sometimes you just don't have one or two objects or photos that would enhance the exhibition. In most cases, though, you can borrow them from another museum or one of your members, or buy them.

Museums are often quite happy to loan back and forth as long as you promise to take good care of the objects you borrow. I recommend starting by calling museums of a similar size to your own. Large museums will have strict standards for object exhibition that you may have trouble meeting, but another museum like your own may have exactly what you are looking for and would be happy to see it displayed.

Internet shopping has made it possible for us to buy just about anything, and if you need a man's suit from around 1910 you can find one. If you get something that has no local history and you don't want to keep it in your collection, put it back on the Internet at the end of the exhibition and sell it to someone else.

Reproductions or replicas can serve an excellent purpose in an exhibition. One benefit of these objects is that you can leave them out as hands-on items. Make sure to label them as modern reproductions so that visitors don't think you are letting people handle your collection.

Determine If the Objects Can Be Safely Displayed

Museums collect objects for two reasons: (1) to preserve them forever, (2) to share them with the public. These reasons directly contradict each other—the conditions that provide perfect preservation do not allow display and vice versa. In her article on exhibition environments for collections, Heather Maximea stated:

> At the heart of many museum exhibition projects is the use of collections of art, artifacts, or specimens. The objects are often irreplaceable resources. . . . As such, their preservation for posterity is of

great importance and is one of the key mandates of the museum enterprise. It is necessary to admit that the display process itself . . . may be detrimental to preservation, since they may expose the objects to a less controlled environment, and thus to higher levels of light, dust, pollutants. Reducing the extent to which the exhibition facilities cause these physical hazards to the collection is a key goal of the building and exhibition design process. (Maximea, 2014: 61)

General Room Conditions

It is easy to keep in mind that if you are comfortable in a room, the objects probably are, too. You don't have to spend a fortune to protect your museum's collection.

When people donate objects to your museum, they trust you to take good care of them. The National Park Service has created a *Museum Handbook* that is available online, and states that the main causes of deterioration to your collection are light, temperature, relative humidity, and contaminants (National Park Service, 2016: 4:2).

Light: sunlight is the most awful thing you can expose your objects to. The National Park Service *Museum Handbook* tells us that "even small amounts of light will cause damage to most materials. The rate of damage is proportional to the illumination level multiplied by the time of exposure. Therefore, it is essential for you to determine how much exposure an object on exhibit should be subjected to, and over what period of time" (National Park Service, 2016: 4:43). That's why museums don't allow flash photography in the exhibition spaces. One single flash can equal years of sunlight. Visitors will tell you "Oh, it's OK. It's a digital camera," but that doesn't make a difference. It's the flash that matters, not the medium that the image is stored on.

Temperature: food keeps better in the refrigerator, and so do photos and clothing. You also know that metal expands in heat—that's why you can get the lid off a jar if you put the lid under hot water for a minute. At the same time, other types of materials contract in heat. As the National Park Service *Museum Handbook* reminds us: "Temperature fluctuations can cause materials to expand and contract rapidly, setting up destructive stresses on the object. Fluctuations that occur faster than an object's ability to adjust to the change are most likely to cause damage such as cracking or exfoliating. . . . Rapid variations can cause more problems than the specific level" (National Park Service, 2016: 4:22). Extreme temperatures are detrimental for most organic materials. Antique furniture is often held together by horse glue, which will soften in heat and contract in cold, thus causing the laminate and joints to detach.

Humidity: you probably know of a door that never closes well on a hot, humid day because the wood has soaked up moisture in the air and expanded. Humidity can have even worse effects on artifacts than heat. Paper, fabrics, wood, and other organic materials can swell and shrink with moisture gain and loss. The NPS *Museum Handbook* states: "All organic materials and some inorganic materials absorb and give off water depending on the RH [relative humidity] of the surrounding air. Effects of RH on objects include: faster corrosion of metal objects at higher RH, pests and mold growth are more common at higher RH, shrinking and cracking in organic materials can occur at low RH" (National Park Service, 2016: 4:9).

So you can see that the one piece of equipment your museum really needs is an HVAC unit—heat and air conditioning. Fortunately, many agencies that give grants understand how important this is. A side benefit is that your visitors will be more comfortable too, and will spend more time (and money) in your museum. Once you have finished this exhibition, your next project assignment is to write a grant for an HVAC unit.

What Will People See?

Specific Artifact Conditions

No matter how much care your museum takes to preserve artifacts, some objects are very fragile. It's happened to me more times than I like to think about. My records indicate that I have a flag, banner, or skirt from the right time period. It will be perfect for the exhibition. So I go to the box, put on my gloves, open the lid, and gently start to lift it out. The fabric makes a noise that indicates it is falling apart. I immediately, but gently, set it back down into the box. That item will not go on display.

The Smithsonian spent millions of dollars to get a backing sewn on the Star-Spangled Banner and a special display case designed with temperature control and low light levels. Most of us do not have that option. You will have to make the decision to display the object, knowing that it will never be the same, to completely remove it from the exhibition, or to display some facsimile such as a photo or replica.

Learning from Experience: A museum I worked at had a document with the original signature of a U.S. president from the early 1800s. The document had been displayed in light for many years before being donated to the museum, and the signature was faint. Any more light damage might destroy it completely. In that case, I took a photograph (with no flash) of the document and displayed the copy. Of course, it was labeled as a copy. Visitors would prefer to see the actual document, but in this situation the copy was the only option. The museum got a few requests from visitors to see the original, and they were taken into the collection area to view it.

Photographs and Drawings

Images of objects being used can bring those artifacts to life for people. While it is nice to see a carpenter's drawing knife, you gain a better appreciation of it if you see an image of a carpenter holding it in both hands and drawing it toward him. Now visitors can see how it works and look at the knife with deeper understanding. Small museum experts Eugene Dillenburg and Janice Klein explain in *Small Museum Toolkit 5*:

> Photographs can show objects or activities that are too large to fit in a case, or even the museum, such as an image of a Hopi woman replastering her adobe home or a Civil War cannon. Photographs can also take the place of objects that may be unavailable or beyond the museum's resources to display properly, but that are key to the story line, like an image of a woman in full Victorian dress. (Dillenburg and Klein, 2012: 80)

On the other hand, you don't want your entire exhibition to be photos. People come to museums to see real objects. If, for some reason, you have a project based on photos, you have two choices: make this project a book rather than an exhibition, or find objects to accompany the images.

Learning from Experience: A museum received an extensive collection of local postcards as a donation. The gift had great monetary as well as historical significance. The museum director wanted to mount an exhibition of the postcards. But a display of hundreds of flat postcards would get boring very quickly. So while many postcards were put into exhibit cases, some were blown up to various sizes and put on wall panels. Actual objects representing items in the postcard images were placed in exhibit cases or between the images. In this photo you see a recreation of the Tea Room that was featured in a postcard, between panels with the enlarged images and text.

Image 4.1 Tearoom and postcard exhibit.

Copyright

Most images have copyright protection. Legally, if you copy an image out of a book and use it in your exhibition, you need the permission of the publisher. Your exhibit labels should give credit to any other museum or publication that you borrow images from.

There are very few exceptions to this rule. These are:

1. Your own collection. Your donation form should indicate that the donor hands over the copyright (if it doesn't, make sure you add it). You own those images and the copyright to them.

2. Library of Congress. You, as an American, own those images. However, you should still credit the library in your labels.

3. Copyright-free images and clip art. These are easily accessible on the Internet, or you can buy CDs of clip art at most art supply stores. You may even have books lying around your museum office with clip art images.

4. Antique Sears and Roebucks catalogs. In fact, images from any catalog produced before 1920 can be used, but you should still credit the source.

Now that you've started thinking about it, this is the time for you to do the research in your collection and make a preliminary list of the objects and photos you may possibly want to use. Exhibit Worksheet 5: Objects and Photos will help you through this process. Then we'll start the next section on the appearance of the exhibition.

Worksheet 5

EXHIBIT WORKSHEET 5: OBJECTS AND PHOTOS

EXHIBIT TOPIC: _____

OBJECTS FROM OUR COLLECTION:

Accession #	Object Name	Year	Relevance
_____	_____	_____	_____
_____	_____	_____	_____
_____	_____	_____	_____
_____	_____	_____	_____
_____	_____	_____	_____
_____	_____	_____	_____
_____	_____	_____	_____

Continue on another paper

OBJECTS WE'D LIKE TO BORROW/BUY:

_____

Continue on another paper

PHOTOS FROM OUR COLLECTION:

_____	_____	_____	_____
_____	_____	_____	_____
_____	_____	_____	_____
_____	_____	_____	_____
_____	_____	_____	_____
_____	_____	_____	_____

Continue on another paper

Mood/Visitor Experience

You will want your exhibition to set a mood. This is the section for the design and installation volunteers, or it is time for the solo exhibition developer to put on the design hat. Now you get to play with colors and lights and furniture arranging.

Is the topic toys? Then the mood should be sunny and playful. Is the topic funerals? Then the mood should be subdued and somber. Is the topic local fish? Maybe you want to give an underwater feel.

Every aspect of your exhibition will help set the mood. The colors of the walls and exhibit cases, the font used in your labels, and the arrangement of the panels and cases will all be important components of getting your visitors into the right frame of mind for your exhibition.

Color

Color is very important. There are many great resources for using color in interior decorating, and they apply to exhibitions as well. *Small Museum Toolkit 5* advises: "Bright primary colors create very different effects than light pastels or deep, dramatic shades. Cases painted to blend in with the floor or walls can make a small space look bigger" (Dillenburg and Klein, 2012: 87).

According to museum graphic designer Jacqueline Tang, "Color plays a major role in how a design is perceived by its audience. As we know, color is often associated with temperature or moods. . . . Color can also play an organizational role in the exhibition . . . differentiating between thematic areas or zones in the gallery" (Tang, 2014: 316).

One of the best investments you can make is in a paint chip sample book, which you can purchase at any paint store. Since you are a nonprofit, you can also ask if they will donate one to you. Your exhibition team can look at exact colors and select the specific ones they want. You can take your colors to the paint store and get those exact colors so there will be no confusion or surprises when the walls are done.

While art museums often prefer to paint their walls plain white, bright colors can benefit exhibitions of history, natural history, and science. Kathleen McLean wrote in *Planning for People in Museum Exhibitions*: "Color can be used in many different ways in an exhibit. It can be a major factor in creating a cultural context, or it can be employed primarily for emphasis and highlighting of important components and information" (McLean, 1993: 132).

One important aspect to consider is the size of the room. Most exhibition spaces are much larger than living rooms, so you can use bolder colors than you would at home. If your hardware store has good employees at the paint counter, they may ask you, "Are you sure you want to paint the room this color?" They are right—you would not want to paint your own home walls Harvest Gold and Avacado Green, but they are the perfect colors for an exhibition on the 1970s.

> **Learning from Experience:** One museum decided to do something different from their usual bright colors and painted the walls white for an exhibition. Visitors and board members complained that it was the most boring exhibition the museum had ever done. They never mentioned the wall color, they just said the whole exhibition was blah. After a few weeks the curator went out and bought three-foot-wide bright pink dots to stick on the walls and painted trim on the exhibit cases to match. The complaints stopped.

Choose one main color and then select a complimentary color for each section of the exhibit. Color cues are important to visitors, as a change in the color of the labels and cases tells people they have entered a new section of the exhibition (McLean, 1993: 132). Even if they don't see the title panel for the new section, they will subconsciously register the new color as a change.

Music

In a silent room, people will tend to whisper. Your visitors will feel much more comfortable talking aloud to each other if there is some background noise. Whether you play ocean sounds or music, do plan to have some soundtrack to your exhibition. For a historic exhibition, play some music of the era. Put on a CD. Put up a sign telling people what they are listening to, and sell the CD in your gift shop. The American Society of Composers, Authors, and Publishers (ASCAP) allows the use of radio or recorded music in a nonprofit setting if "there is no admission charge, or if there is a charge, all proceeds after deduction of costs are used exclusively for educational, religious or charitable purposes" (http://www.ascap.com).

Hands-On Activities

Most people think of hands-on activities as being for kids, but experience will show you that just as many adults use them.

Hands-on components can be incorporated into the exhibition or can be separated into their own area, or a combination of both.

Plan on testing your interactive components and making changes to them as time goes on since they are the part of an exhibition most likely not to be understood by visitors. They are also susceptible to damage over time, so always buy multiples of any item crucial to the hands-on activity.

I will provide more details on construction in the "How Will We Do It?" chapter of this book, but here are some ideas to get you started.

Low Tech

The easiest hands-on activity is to set an object on a table and allow people to pick it up and examine it. You will want to use a replica or duplicate item as it is not wise to put objects from your collection out to be handled. I am very sorry to tell you that they will get damaged or even stolen. Be sure to put out a sign telling people what the object is and that it is fine to touch it.

> Museum objects, for all their glory, can generally only be viewed, not touched or moved. Touchable components engage more of visitors' senses and thus more of their brains. Nonaccessioned objects or modern-day replicas placed on "touching tables" are the most common and simplest type of hands-on materials. . . . Clearly identifying these as noncollection items helps visitors understand that the museum maintains appropriate standards for the care of its collection and does not allow accessioned objects to be handled. (Dillenburg and Klein, 2012: 80)

Activities that people can move or manipulate in some way are technically called *interactives*. For purposes of this book, we will use the term *hands-on* for anything that people can handle. If you set up an activity for people to engage in, make sure it resets itself. Or be sure to plan to have a volunteer/staff person on hand to reset it as needed. If people will lift a flap to see an answer, have it lift up from the bottom so it will fall closed. If you set out a home weaving kit, plan time to undo the weaving every night at closing.

Interactive components, which have the visitor do something, like press a button or lift a flap, work best when the activity itself reinforces the message. For example, putting flappers over a picture of the local environment and posing the question "Where do hummingbirds live?" makes lifting the flappers an act of searching, which is exactly what a naturalist trying to answer the question would do. The activity becomes part of the answer. (Dillenburg and Klein, 2012: 81)

Museum Toolkit 5 goes on to advise small museums that "interactives do not have to be expensive." Some simple examples include:

- Graphics mounted on boards that slide past one another

- Overlays printed on acrylic

- Oversize maps laid out on the floor

- Models to put together

- Drawers that open to reveal additional objects

- Mounted magnifying glasses showing detail of small objects (Dillenburg and Klein, 2012: 81)

High Tech

Remember—people come to museums to see the real things. They can play with computers at home. Kathleen McLean, a museum exhibition consultant, wrote, "We have the real things. It is the interactions among people, real objects, phenomena, and ideas that make museum exhibitions unique. Exhibitions are the essence of a museum experience" (McLean, 1993: 15).

Having said that, there are always exciting new technological gadgets and techniques that can enhance an exhibition: you can show a looping video, play sounds at the touch of a button, project images, or send information to the visitors' own devices.

Because technology is constantly changing, I will refer you to the Internet, including the website for this book, for the latest information. Seek out some children or teens for advice on what young folks in your area are using.

You do not have to decide exactly what hands-on activities you want at this point in your planning—just decide if you want to include them and where you would like to place them.

Room Layout

Now that you have decided what objects you will display, you can begin to think about your room layout. If you find that the exhibition will include many images, you will need a lot of walls. If you find it will be mostly objects, you will need more exhibit cases.

Visitors enjoy being able to wander around and look at exhibit cases from multiple sides. In addition, the room looks fuller and more interesting when there are cases in the middle of the room. "Rather than placing cases or components around the perimeter of the room, wherever possible create a path that allows visitors to walk between them" (Dillenberg and Klein, 2012: 87).

Exhibition spaces can be organized in a few basic ways: linear, radial, and random floor plans (McLean, 1993: 125). Of course, professional designers can come up with many other types, but these three are a good start.

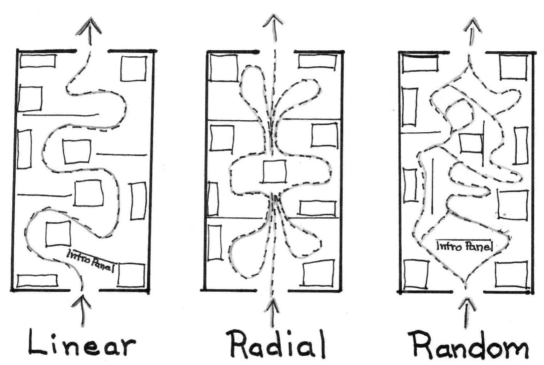

Image 4.2 The same pieces of exhibit furniture and walls were used to create these three different floor plans.

Linear Floor Plan

Linear designs use the cases and temporary walls to create a path that visitors must follow. This plan is used for exhibitions intended to be seen in a particular order. These might include animal life cycles or history stories. If the order is important, you will want to build the visitors' pathway to gently guide them the way you want them to go. Museum visitor studies experts John Falk and Lynn Dierking report that decades of study have confirmed "the tendency of visitors to turn to the right upon entering a gallery" (Falk and Dierking, 2013: 132).

If you want visitors to start the exhibition by going to the left, you have to make it impossible to go right. Timelines are usually read left to right, so exhibitions that follow a timeline will want to encourage visitors to move in that direction.

Radial Floor Plan

Radial designs are created around a hub in the center, such as a central object that the exhibition is based around. For example, if the theme is turtles, there may be a large fiberglass turtle in the middle, or even a tank of live turtles. Then each of the spaces radiating off of the center covers some aspect of the theme. Again, using turtles, various side spaces may be about turtle reproduction, turtle food, turtle hibernation, and more. Likewise, if the theme is wagon trains, a large wagon in the middle could be surrounded by sections on what people took with them, the dangers they faced, why they made the trip, and other details.

Random Floor Plan

Most visitors prefer a random exhibition floor plan since this allows them to wander around as they please. Exhibitions in this category might be highlighting various sections of town, looking at various areas of life (home, work, play), or showing many of the wildlife in the area. With those subjects, it doesn't matter which ones visitors look at first. Kathleen McLean wrote, "No matter how the designer plans for a specific traffic flow, people will go where they want, when they want. To some extent, however, traffic flow depends on the configuration of the space, walls, display furniture, and the location of entrances and exits in the exhibition. Studies have shown that most people turn to their right when entering a gallery, and most people make a direct path through the exhibition from the entrance to the exit. But this is certainly not a fixed rule" (McLean, 1993: 123).

You must assume that visitors will bounce back and forth through your exhibition space and not look at every single case or panel. "Of primary importance is an easy-to-follow story line with each case or component telling a self-contained part of the whole narrative. This allows visitors to take different paths through the exhibit space without confusion" (Dillenburg and Klein, 2012: 87).

ADA Compliance

No matter how you lay out the room, it is important to remember to make the space accessible to everyone. You will have visitors with walkers or wheelchairs. Guidelines from the ADA (Americans with Disabilities Act) are constantly being updated, so use the Department of Justice's ADA website for the most current requirements for museums.

Historic sites must comply with ADA regulations. A wheelchair requires a pathway thirty-six inches wide. The Department of Justice explains that "if people must travel between stanchions or between a wall and a stanchion, passage must be maintained at a minimum of 36 inches wide, measured from inside edge to inside edge of the stanchion bases or floor moldings, except at doors where the width may narrow to 32 inches for a maximum distance of two feet" (ADA.gov, 2009). More room is needed if the wheelchair needs to make a tight turn.

There are also requirements for assisting people who are blind, deaf, or have a number of other disabilities. The U.S. government has kindly provided guidelines just for museums, which can be accessed at http://www.ada.gov/business/museum_access.htm.

Make a Model

It will be well worth your time to make a scale model of your exhibition space. Uncounted hours of work will be saved by looking at a three-dimensional model of a planned exhibition layout and realizing that it won't work. It is much easier to move models of cases than actual cases! You will use this again and again for every exhibition you plan.

Floor Plan

A scale drawing is a good place to start, as it can be useful for the first step in planning your exhibition. I'm sure you remember having to make scale drawings in school, or you've made drawings of your living room and furniture. To get started, get some graph paper and a tape measure. Be sure to include the location and size of walls, windows, doors, and electrical outlets. Museum facilities planner Heather Maximea reminds us that the location of an electrical outlet may be important to the placement of an exhibit case with lighting (Maximea, 2014: 79).

You will also want to measure your exhibit cases and temporary walls. Cut them out of graph paper, and you can move them around on your floor plan, just as if you were arranging furniture for your house. Be sure to store them in an envelope between uses.

If you don't have any exhibit cases yet, this exercise will help you decide what you need.

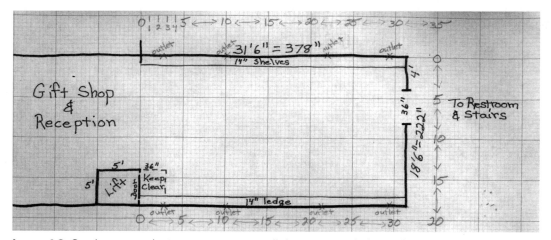

Image 4.3 Graph paper and a tape measure were all that were needed to make this scale drawing of the exhibit space.

Make many copies of your drawing and use them to plan out your exhibition. Where will you put each section of the exhibition (from your outline)? Which sections require more space? More exhibit cases? More wall space? How will visitors flow through the exhibition? Where will you put hands-on activities?

Model

Nothing beats having an actual three-dimensional model. Sometimes a plan looks great on the flat floor plan drawing yet becomes clearly undesirable once it is set up in the model. You probably have some volunteer who is a retired engineer or architect, or a model train enthusiast who would love to build a model for you. If you don't know anyone now, list it in your next newsletter: "Volunteer wanted to build a model of our exhibition hall." You may want to do it yourself. Making the model is easier than you think, and it's a good way to get your creative juices flowing.

You'll want a copy of your floor plan, some foam core (available at any crafts store), glue, a utility knife, and either straight pins or toothpicks. You will also need to measure the heights of your walls, doors, and windows. It is important to note the locations of light switches, too, to make sure you leave the space open.

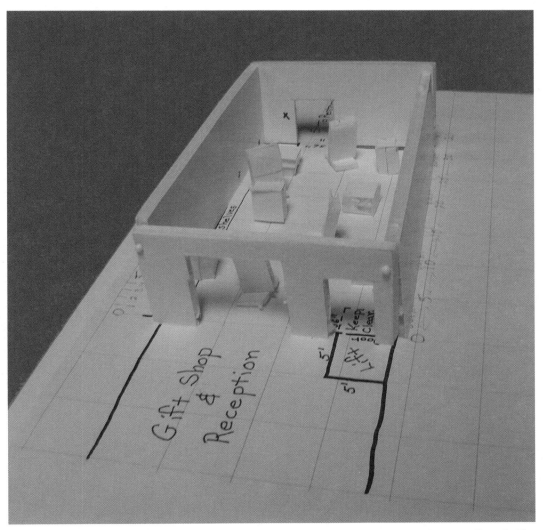

Image 4.4 A model of your exhibit space is the best way to make sure the room layout will work. The furniture models can be crudely made, so long as they are the right scale size.

Instructions for making a three-dimensional model:

- Lay your floorplan on a flat piece of foam core and glue it down.

- Cut out the foam core about 3 inches larger than the floor plan on all sides.

- Draw each wall and cut it out of the foam core. Mark outlets, switches, and other features.

- Insert the pins or toothpicks into the floor plan from the bottom. Lay down a line of glue, and place your walls upright on your floor.

- While the glue is drying, you can cut out your exhibit cases and temporary walls.

Conclusion

Now you can feel like you are starting to put together a real exhibition. Make copies of the scale drawing of your floor plan, bring your object worksheets and your paint chip sample book, and gather your committee, or take yourself out for coffee. Begin to envision your exhibition space transformed into an intriguing and informative exhibition.

Worksheet 6

EXHIBIT WORKSHEET 6: EXHIBIT SECTIONS

EXHIBIT TOPIC: _____

MOOD OF THE EXHIBIT: _____

MAIN COLOR: _____

TYPE OF FLOOR PLAN: _____

DRAW A ROUGH DIAGRAM OF THE ROOM LAYOUT ON THE BACK

EXHIBIT SECTION 1 TOPIC: _____

SECONDARY COLOR: _____

OBJECTS THAT HELP TELL THIS STORY: _____

_____

_____

_____

PHOTOS THAT HELP TELL THIS STORY: _____

_____

_____

HANDS-ON ACTIVITIES: _____

EXHIBIT SECTION 2 TOPIC: _____

SECONDARY COLOR: _____

OBJECTS THAT HELP TELL THIS STORY: _____

_____

_____

_____

PHOTOS THAT HELP TELL THIS STORY: _____

_____

_____

HANDS-ON ACTIVITIES: _____

EXHIBIT SECTION 3 TOPIC: _____

SECONDARY COLOR: _____

OBJECTS THAT HELP TELL THIS STORY: _____

_____

_____

_____

PHOTOS THAT HELP TELL THIS STORY: _____

_____

_____

HANDS-ON ACTIVITIES: _____

To-Do List

Buy a paint chip sample book.

Fill out Exhibit Worksheet 5: Objects and Photos.

Draw a floor plan of your exhibition space and furniture.

Make a model of your exhibition space and furniture.

Make copies of Exhibit Worksheet 6: Exhibit Sections.

Fill out copies of Exhibit Worksheet 6: Exhibit Sections.

Check the additional resources on our website.

Sources

American Society of Composers, Authors, and Publishers. "Using Copyrighted Music." Accessed June 2016. http://www.ascap.com/~/media/655449c494b748ba89edc4864655e1b6.pdf.

Dillenburg, Eugene, and Janice Klein. "Creating Exhibits: From Planning to Building." In *Small Museum Toolkit 5, Interpretation: Education, Programs, and Exhibits.* Edited by Cinnamon Catlin-Legutko and Stacy Klingler, 71–97. New York: Rowman & Littlefield, 2012.

Falk, John H., and Lynn D. Dierking. *The Museum Experience Revisited.* Walnut Creek, CA: Left Coast Press, 2013.

Maximea, Heather. "Exhibition Facilities." In *Manual of Museum Exhibitions, Second Edition.* Edited by Barry Lord and Maria Piacente, 57–98. New York: Rowman & Littlefield, 2014.

McLean, Kathleen. *Planning for People in Museum Exhibitions.* Washington, DC: Association of Science-Technology Centers, 1993.

National Park Service. *Museum Handbook, Part I Museum Collections.* National Park Service, 2016.

Tang, Jacqueline. "Graphic Design." In *Manual of Museum Exhibitions, Second Edition.* Edited by Barry Lord and Maria Piacente, 314–21. New York: Rowman & Littlefield, 2014.

United States Department of Justice, Civil Rights Division. "Maintaining Accessibility in Museums." 2009. Accessed 2016. http://www.ada.gov/business/museum_access.htm.

Chapter 5
What Will We Tell Them?

Label Writing

Exhibit labels tell your visitors what they are looking at, but, more importantly, labels are what make your collection of things a museum exhibit. Visitors want to know what the objects are, how old they are, who used them, what they were used for, and so on. Otherwise, they could have just gone shopping and seen interesting objects that they could pick up and handle, and maybe even take home.

Personally, I find label writing to be fun, fascinating, frustrating, and fulfilling. As you work to make your exhibition great, you will find yourself often making changes to the labels, even after the exhibition has opened. That's as it should be—you will be constantly responding to visitor feedback.

Beverly Serrell is probably the field's foremost expert in writing interpretive labels. She has been studying labels since the 1980s, and I consider her my personal role model for this process. In her preface to the second edition of her book *Exhibit Labels*, she wrote:

• Labels are really important, even in this digital age.

• They can be done right, and it's worth it.

• It takes a lot of time and hard work to get them right.

• Words work better with supporting visuals and vice versa.

• Evaluation is mandatory for interactive exhibit labels. (Serrell, 2015: x)

 So gather up your curatorial and education volunteers, or get your curator and educator hats, and get ready to tell the visitors about your topic.

Museum Visitors versus Book Readers

The most important thing to remember is that people are standing up while reading your labels. They are walking around a room and are probably attracted by the wonderful variety of objects you have presented to them. This means the labels will have to be SHORT.

I know; this hurts. There is so much to tell about every object, and you want your visitors to enjoy it all. But they will only read a short label. If it is long, they will simply move on to the next object and label. Sorry, but it's true.

When I'm working with a new group of volunteers, I always tell them this dinosaur story as reported by Beverly Serrell. The Field Museum of Natural History has a dinosaur exhibit in the main hall. "As an experiment, a 326-word, typewritten label was installed alongside the dinosaurs on a Saturday afternoon. In the text, five lines from the bottom, was inserted the statement 'If you have read this far, please step to the desk marked visitor research and claim a small prize.' . . . During a three-hour period, fourteen people asked for their reward. Several other visitors were observed reading, looking back toward the desk, laughing, and walking away. . . . It was estimated that close to 15 percent of the readers were finishing the entire 326-word label" (Serrell, 1983: 73).

Remember—that label was about dinosaurs, a topic that many people are very interested in. Would even 15 percent read a long label about a different type of object? No. Less is more. Most of the paragraphs in the book you are now reading are short—has that helped make it easier to read?

The good news is that anything you have to leave out of the exhibit label you can put into the auxiliary material—booklet, catalog, website, audio tour, and more. So our mantra will be: "Remember the dinosaur, and the rest goes in the booklet." We'll talk more about this later.

Types of Museum Labels and Signage

There are various types of labels and signs in your museum.

- Wayfinding Signs: Before visitors can enjoy your exhibition, many of them want to find the restroom. (Serrell, 2015: 54)

- Donor/Credit Signs: People and organizations that support your museum can be thanked in a main donor panel. Often museums will list their main donors in a sign near the entrance. A credit sign thanking all the volunteers who worked on the exhibition is good for morale. (Serrell, 2015: 41)

- Exhibition Title Labels: Your exhibition has a title. Put it up in a large sign by the entrance to the exhibition, or as the first thing people see as they enter the exhibition. It helps them understand the context of what they will see. (Serrell, 2015: 32)

- Section Introduction Labels: At each new section of the exhibition you will want to have a title for that section and an introductory paragraph. This label will introduce visitors to the topic for that section. (Serrell, 2015: 35)

- Interpretive Labels: These are the labels you will put next to each object in the exhibition. The rest of this chapter will deal with interpretive labels, also called captions.

Writing Interpretive Labels

I call the object labels *interpretive labels* because they should explain the object, not just identify it. If I read that this object is a portrait painted by a certain artist in a certain year, what have I learned? If I read that the person in this portrait was essential in the founding of my city, lived in that large house on the hill, and hired a certain artist to paint the portrait, now I have learned an interesting story.

A story is easier to remember than facts and makes a stronger impression. Your exhibition and labels need to tell stories. Each object label needs to have a very short story, and each of those should be a part of the larger exhibition story.

Below are concepts you should keep in mind as you write your labels.

Start with the Object

Your visitor is looking at an object and wants the label to explain what it is. So start with the object. "Start with what you can see and build toward a generalization," wrote Beverly Serrell (2015: 173). In your first draft, you can write "This is a . . ." as the first sentence of all your labels, as long as you promise to change most of them before your final draft. Your visitors want some variety in their labels.

Tie into the Big Idea

Remember in chapter 3 when I made you condense your exhibition topic to a sentence? Go get Exhibit Worksheet 4: Exhibit Topic and look at what you wrote. Everything else you write should connect back to that. If you find yourself getting too far off topic, you need to rein yourself in before you find you are starting another exhibition (Serrell, 2015: 12).

Make Sense on Its Own

Visitors will move around your exhibition as they feel like it. They may skip ahead to an object that attracts their attention and then come back to an earlier one. The main point is that they will read your labels out of order, as was mentioned in chapter 3. You must assume that any given label may be the first one they read (Serrell, 2015: 35).

Keep It Short

As you have to cut text, remember the dinosaur—the rest goes in the booklet. (I'm assuming here that you read about the dinosaur earlier in this chapter. This would never work on an exhibit label. It might not even work here—did you read about the dinosaur? It was in the section titled "Museum Visitors versus Book Readers.") Beverly Serrell suggests that the label should be short enough to be read in ten seconds—about fifty words (Serrell, 2015: 37).

Caption the Objects

The idea behind writing your labels is based on *National Geographic* magazines. Think about an article in that magazine. You can go through it the first time reading only the photo captions and get the big idea. Then if you are interested in finding out more, you can read the entire article.

Your photo and object labels are like the photo captions. The Section Introduction Label has already given the context for the story. And if your visitors want a lot more information, where do they go? That's right—the auxiliary materials. Beverly Serrell reminds us that "the best way to provide more information is in a form other than labels such as a brochure, website, or better yet, let them Google it for themselves" (Serrell, 2015: 158).

Use Positive Statements

It is a quirk of the human mind that we tend to block out negative words such as *don't*, *aren't*, and *no*. Psychologists tell us that "consciously we understand that 'Don't forget' means to 'remember' but unconsciously our minds drop the 'don't' and file it as 'forget,' thus conveying the opposite message" (Cognitive Sciences Stack Exchange, 2016). Visitors will remember the words on your label but may sometimes remember the meaning incorrectly.

For example, if you wrote a label that said, "Sharks don't like to eat people," odds are that most visitors would go home and tell their friends that sharks like to eat people.

As you continue reading this book, you may notice that I am using that trick on you. There are very few negative sentences in this book, and definitely none in this paragraph. (Whew. Do you know how hard it was to not write "Don't say *don't*"?)

Target the Audience

You know that all sorts of people will come into your museum, but who did you decide is your target audience for this exhibition? Look at Exhibit Worksheet 4: Exhibit Topic and see what you wrote down, as you will want to keep those people in mind as you write. Make sure that you use age-group-appropriate language and references. Today's fourth-graders don't remember September 11 or know what a cassette tape is, and people new to your town never knew where Fred's Market used to be. Beverly Serrell wrote, "Visitors who are experts are not the target audience for the label copy, and experts (unless they are really snobs) will not be insulted by clear, concise labels that are written with enthusiasm for the subject and a respect for novice visitors" (Serrell, 2015: 96).

Utilize Illustrations as Necessary

Sometimes illustrations or clip art are nice additions to a label, as they can help illustrate how the object was used. For example, it is interesting to see a horse harness, but the object makes much more sense when we see how it fits on the horse. (By the way, antique Sears and Roebucks catalogs are fabulous for this sort of thing, and the oldest ones are copyright-free.) Beverly Serrell wrote that "in the best of all possible situations, when images and words are working well with each other, the words and the images together create a complete experience that neither one could do alone" (Serrell, 2015: 173).

Sample Label-Writing Exercise

Let's try a few sample labels before you get to your actual exhibit objects. We will pick one section of an exhibition and three objects in it. We'll call this section "Twentieth-Century Office Supplies." The big idea is that these items were once vital to an office but are no longer used.

"Twentieth-Century Office Supplies"

Object 1: Calculator

Object 2: Wite-Out

Object 3: Highlighter

Image 5.1 "Twentieth-Century Office Supplies"—calculator from the Federal Courthouse, bottle of Wite-Out, highlighter pen.

For each object write three or four sentences that add up to no more than fifty words. Think about *National Geographic* photo captions, and make them relevant and interesting. I recommend you do the first one, then review it, then the second, and so on. You'll learn from your mistakes better if you do them one at a time.

1. Start with something physical about the object.

    This is a _____.

    The color is because _____.

    This was made out of _____.

2. Tie the object to the exhibition theme.

    These were commonly used for _____.

    This was used on the occasion of _____.

    This was made by _____.

3. Give us one or two fun details.

    If you look closely you can see _____.

    The owner of this particular one said (or did) _____.

    These were rare (or common) because _____.

4. STOP.

    This is the hardest part. You have now written everything most visitors are going to read.

How did that process go for you? Was it hard to stick to just fifty words? Any time your self-control starts to slip and you want to write more, remember the dinosaur.

This first draft needs to be rewritten so that it flows better. Go ahead and write a second draft. I'll wait. Take your time.

Your sample labels might have come out something like this:

Object 1: Draft 1: This is a calculator. It only did math, nothing more. This one has an American flag on it because it was in the Federal Courthouse.

Object 1: Draft 2: Calculators like this were on most office desks in the late twentieth century. They only did basic math and were replaced by computers with built-in calculators. An employee at the Federal Courthouse added an American flag to this one.

If you were a visitor in a museum, would you read that? Would it answer your questions about the object? Repeat this process with the second and then third objects.

Now write a label that might head the section that all of these objects are in. This will introduce visitors to this part of the exhibition and can be a bit longer than an object label—it can have up to seventy-five words (Serrell, 2015: 43).

Your sample section label might have come out something like this:

Twentieth-Century Office Supplies

In the second half of the twentieth century, office workers felt very modern with the equipment available to them. These devices really did make work easier than it had been. Word-processing programs today include calculator, backspace, and highlight features based on these separate objects.

Physical Attributes

Now you get to consider what your labels look like. This will make a difference in whether or not people want to read them. When faced with text that is difficult to read, most people will just ignore it. Visitors are interested in the objects, not the words (Serrell, 2015: 19).

Typeface and Size

There are two basic kinds of typeface, or font: serif or sans serif. A serif font has little curlicues at the starts and ends of letters, usually most easily seen on the bottom of the y and the tip of the c. A sans serif font does not have them ("sans" is French for "without") (Tang, 2014, 315). Experts disagree over which is easier to read and can quote scientific studies to support their views (Thompson and Thompson, 2014, 333). You have a variety of both on your computer.

Easy-to-read serif fonts

Times-Roman

Garamond

Easy-to-read sans serif fonts

Arial

Franklin

The website ScienceBuddies.org has prepared rules for student science fair project boards. These rules also apply to your small museum exhibition design. You can find one example in this book as table 7.1 on page 126.

Text Size

You will want your labels to be large enough for visitors to read. Once again, keep in mind that the visitors are standing up and walking around your exhibition. They need a larger font than you use in a paper you hold in your hand.

When we get to the section on constructing your labels, we will go over this in more detail. But for now, keep in mind that museum experts agree that the smallest point size you should ever use is eighteen. I know that looks large on your paper, but lay it down on a table and back away. It's not really that large, is it? If lights around the label are dim, you may want to make the point size even larger.

You will want even larger point sizes for your titles and section headings. Again, there are more details in the chapter on printing and mounting labels.

Donor/Loaner/Accession Information

At the very bottom of your label, in smaller print than everything else, will be the museum accession number and the name of the loaner or donor. I know your donors want to see their names nice and large, but do you think your out-of-town visitors care? It's like the credits at the end of a movie. As Kermit the Frog said in the *Muppet Movie*, "Sure, someone reads the credits. Those people have families."

Do yourself a favor and include the accession number. There are a number of reasons for this: someone may ask you for more information about the object and you can easily look it up, you may want to re-create the exhibition someday and you will know which label went with which object, or someone may want to know about that teapot you had in the exhibition three years ago.

Colors

You will want to use a color (or colors) that coordinates with your exhibition colors. Section titles, especially, can use the background color to signify to visitors that this information goes with the new section of the exhibition.

Just remember to keep the paper or background color very light. You want the text to stand out against the paper. If your wall color is royal blue, use baby blue paper for your labels. Within exhibit cases, keep most of the labels on white paper. You will probably use a white background within the case, also. As Beverly Serrell wrote, "Regardless of the choice or combination of colors, the most important thing is contrast" (Serrell, 2015: 275).

Aging and Disabilities

Remember that as people age their eyes change and they have trouble distinguishing things that have a similar brightness. People with diminished eyesight have the same problem. Museum education specialist Tamerra Moeller wrote, "Any printed material should have large print against a non-glare background, and the color of the print should contrast with the paper on which it is printed. Black print on a beige or off-white background, or red print on a yellow background would be preferable" (Moeller, 1984: 8).

When lights glare on a label, the words are difficult to read. This is especially true for people with vision problems and for people in wheelchairs who are lower than standing eye level. Reduce the use of direct lighting (which isn't good for the artifacts, anyway), and don't put labels in plexiglass unless you absolutely have to (Thompson and Thompson, 2014: 332). When we get to actually installing the exhibition, we'll talk about ways to mount labels.

Visitors with limited vision will find it easier to read labels when there is "a strong contrast between print and background" (Thompson and Thompson, 2014: 333). Color-blind people cannot see the difference between red and green. If the light is dim, make the font sizes larger.

Sample Label

Your sample label should have large, clear lettering with just a few short sentences. It will include the object number and the donor information.

Sample Finished Label
Calculator

Calculators like this were on most office desks in the late 20th century. Once computers with built-in calculators became common, this piece of equipment was retired. An employee at the Federal Courthouse added an American flag to this one.

Our Museum collection 1989.003.0005   Donated by Jane & John Doe

---

You are now ready to fill out Exhibit Worksheet 7: Label and Signage Appearance, which will record your decisions about the label colors and text font.

Worksheet 7

EXHIBIT WORKSHEET 7: LABEL AND SIGNAGE APPEARANCE

EXHIBIT TITLE:

EXHIBIT COLORS:

LABEL BACKGROUND COLORS:

    SECTION 1

    SECTION 2

    SECTION 3

    SECTION 4

TYPEFACE:

Auxiliary Materials

There will have been lots of heart-breaking decisions about what to cut from the exhibit labels. You can now heal those wounds by placing the lost stories in auxiliary materials. Beverly Serrell reminds us: "All of these supplemental forms of interpretation will allow interpretive labels to remain brief, as they should be" (Serrell, 2015: 45). Any object or idea that does not relate directly to the big idea belongs in the auxiliary material.

Depending on the resources available, you may want to make a handout, a companion booklet, or a page on your website. If this is a permanent exhibition, you can consider adding an audio tour or developing an app that visitors can access on their own phones. As with most museum topics, there are entire books on these auxiliary methods of distributing information. I will only touch on them here.

Handout

If there is one topic that you think visitors may want to know more about right then and there in the exhibition space, you can easily print out a one-page handout. You can also use this as an opportunity to invite the visitor to sign up for membership and to check your website for future events and exhibitions.

Booklet or Catalog

One of the nice things about an exhibition booklet is that you can create it yourself, print it for little cost, and sell it as a souvenir. Visitors who enjoyed the exhibition, and whose families or artifacts are featured in it, enjoy a low-cost memento that they can take home.

Most computers today come with software that will allow you to create booklets. You can add photos and lay out pages yourself. Publisher, Pages, and LibreOffice are examples of programs you can use. Once you have designed the document, you can take it to a printer or office supply store and get it printed. Be sure to sell the copies for at least twice what they cost you to make.

Image 5.2 These were created on the museum's computer and printed at a local copy store.

Website

Your museum's own website is a logical place to put more information about your exhibition. When you send visitors to your website, you also expose them to your calendar of events, mission statement, and volunteer opportunities.

One of the things I like best about a website is that I can change anything at any time. I can make my writing clearer, answer frequently asked questions, and add new research as it becomes available.

If you don't have a website, talk to your county tourism or chamber of commerce about giving you a page on their website. You really need to be present on the web.

There are many software packages that allow you to create your own webpages without any knowledge about how to program. Ask a high school student about this year's latest and greatest software.

While you are talking to high school students, we should mention that many school districts require students to do community service or service learning as a requirement of graduation. The guidance counselors at your local school can tell you how to get students to volunteer to create a webpage for your latest exhibition.

Audio Tour

Audio tours are no longer reserved for large museums with huge budgets. Today there is a constant stream of new companies popping up with new technology to help you make your own. As of the day I am writing this, tours can be offered through the visitor's own cell phone, but as you are reading it, all of that will probably be out of date.

If you don't think you have anyone who can write and/or read a compelling script, turn to your local community theater or school drama department. They might do it in exchange for advertising for their productions. I know I wouldn't mind hearing: "This audio tour was written and produced by Small Town Community Theater. We produce three plays a year at the Auditorium, and we hope you will come to see our shows."

Apps and Other Technology

"Digital handheld devices with audio, multimedia, apps, interactive games, video, and links to the Internet serve as important secondary sources of information. Screens—inviting more information, media, games, and more—often take more time and attention than visitors are willing to allocate to them in an exhibition," wrote Beverly Serrell (Serrell, 2015: 205).

The fast-changing world of technology offers opportunities for you to present additional information on devices that you provide or on the visitors' own devices. Phones, tables, pads, and very soon probably brain implants allow you to share more details than you can fit into an exhibit label. Again, talk to a teenager about what is available this week.

If you decide to go with an app that downloads onto the visitors' own devices, or something like a CR code that visitors can scan with their own devices, keep in mind that not everyone will have that capability. There will always be people who do not have the latest technology, so you will need to provide an alternative way to access the information.

What Will We Tell Them? **51**

Learning from Experience: I was recently in a large museum while on vacation. There were signs in the lobby telling you about an app you can download to your phone. This app will give you additional information about objects on exhibit and expand background information about exhibition topics. I was at that museum on the last day of my vacation, and I had taken many photos on the trip. You can guess what happened—when I tried to load the app, I got a message that there was not sufficient memory on my phone. I had three options: erase photos, leave the museum and find a store that sold larger memory cards, or do without the app. I decided to do without. The rest of my day in the museum, I kept seeing signs telling me I could learn more about this and that on the app. The more of those signs I saw, the grumpier I became. If the data had been available on their website through their Wi-Fi connection, I could have accessed it.

Worksheet 8

EXHIBIT WORKSHEET 8: INTERPRETIVE LABEL CHECKLIST

Use this checklist for each label you write.

EXHIBIT BIG IDEA:

OBJECT/PHOTO TO BE LABELED:

DOES THIS LABEL:

    START WITH THE OBJECT?

    TIE INTO THE BIG IDEA?

    MAKE SENSE ON ITS OWN?

    KEEP IT SHORT? (50 words)

    LAYER THE INFORMATION?

    USE POSITIVE STATEMENTS?

    TARGET THE AUDIENCE?

Remember the dinosaur!

Conclusion

While you are preparing your exhibition, talk to people about the objects you want to feature. Ask your volunteers what they want to know about the objects. Think about why the objects were selected to be exhibited and what is important about them. Become a label writer in your head.

As you learn how to write labels, use Exhibit Worksheet 8: Interpretive Label Checklist. Make a copy of it for each label you will write. The first few labels you write may take a bit of time, but it is important that you work through each step.

Eventually, the process will become easier. You will be able to sit down and write out your first drafts in a relatively short time. It's those second, third, and fourth drafts that you will spend the rest of your life perfecting. You will learn to appreciate what a good friend the big idea can be. Welcome to the world of interpretive labels—it's actually quite intriguing, and I think you'll be happy to have entered.

To-Do List

Fill out Exhibit Worksheet 7: Label and Signage Appearance.

Do sample label worksheets.

Write sample labels.

Make lots of copies of Exhibit Worksheet 8: Interpretive Label Checklist.

Explore the Internet for websites that accompany exhibitions.

Sources

Cognitive Sciences Stack Exchange. "Is It Better to Say 'Don't Forget' or 'Remember' in Written Encouragement?" Accessed 2016. http://cogsci.stackexchange.com/questions/7804/is-it-better-to-say-dont-forget-or-remember-in-written-encouragement.

Moeller, Tamerra P. "Sensory Changes in Older Adults: Implications for Museums." Museum Education *Roundtable Reports* 9, no. 4 (Fall 1984): 6–8.

Science Buddies. "Science Fair Projects—Project Display Board Fonts." Accessed 2016. http://www.sciencebuddies.org/science-fair-projects/project_display_board_fonts.shtml.

Serrell, Beverly. *Making Exhibit Labels: A Step-by-Step Guide*. Nashville, TN: American Association for State and Local History, 1983.

Serrell, Beverly. *Exhibit Labels, An Interpretive Approach, Second Edition*. New York: Rowman & Littlefield, 2015.

Tang, Jacqueline. "Graphic Design." In *Manual of Museum Exhibitions, Second Edition*. Edited by Barry Lord and Maria Piacente, 314–21. New York: Rowman & Littlefield, 2014.

Thompson, Craig, and Philip Thompson. "Universal Design and Diversity." In *Manual of Museum Exhibitions, Second Edition*. Edited by Barry Lord and Maria Piacente, 322–34. New York: Rowman & Littlefield, 2014.

Chapter 6

Will It Work?

Testing exhibit mock-ups allows you to take the concepts of the exhibition team and polish them to make them shine. This is the chapter museum staff and volunteers are most likely to skip because it takes time and sounds tedious. But it is possible that you might actually enjoy this process. It is certain that you will save yourself time, money, and embarrassment if you go through it, so give evaluation a chance and at least keep reading a bit longer.

There is only one way to find out if your visitors will understand your exhibits, and that is to try them out. If you ever go to a museum conference or read a museum studies textbook, you will hear over and over again the word *evaluate*. There is good reason for this—museums want to ensure that their exhibits are "working" as planned, as well as if visitors understand and enjoy the exhibits. Granting agencies often want to know this too and require evaluation of projects they fund. John Falk and Lynn Dierking have made a career of studying visitor experiences in museums, and they point out that "a little investment in front-end and formative evaluation pays huge dividends down the road by helping to avoid expensive mistakes and miscalculations, and investment in summative/outcome assessment is the tool museums need to convince funders that museums truly matter" (Falk and Dierking, 2013: 306).

There are professionals who do nothing but provide evaluation services for museums. They know how to study visitors and have written entire books on the topic. Since you probably have to do this yourself while you are building the exhibition, we will keep to the basics.

Just about everyone in your committee can be involved in this process. You can pull in the talents of a variety of people to get the best results possible. You will especially need your curatorial, education, design, and installation volunteers involved (or your hats ready to put on).

Evaluation

Evaluation is a simple process of asking visitors their opinions. You will discover that people like to be asked, and that they will serve as publicity agents for your museum by telling their friends about their sneak preview of a new exhibition.

There are three phases of museum exhibition evaluation, each building on the other:

- Front end: audience research to determine their interest and knowledge as part of the process of selecting an exhibition topic

- Formative: tests of the planned design and text for understandability

- Summative: measure the success of the exhibition at educating the visitors (Grewcock, 2014: 34–35)

You did front-end evaluation back in chapter 3. You thought about who your visitors were, and you may have done a member or visitor survey to find out what they would like to see exhibited. So you are already one-third done with the evaluation process.

Now it's time to do formative evaluation. *Planning for People in Museum Exhibitions* author Kathleen McLean tells us:

> Formative evaluation . . . focuses on ways to improve and refine an exhibition during its development. . . . mockups and simulations are tested with sample audiences. Through the use of questionnaires and informal, open-ended interviews, formative evaluation can tell planners how to adjust and revise an exhibition so that it conveys and does what is intended. Formative evaluation helps determine conceptual clarity (do people get it?), visitor motivations and behaviors (will people want to use the exhibit and know what to do?), and in the case of an interactive exhibit, mechanical and structural feasibility (will it work the way it's supposed to?). (McLean, 1993: 73)

Basically, formative evaluation lets you know if visitors will understand your exhibit and learn the things you wanted them to learn. The only way to find out is to ask them (Soren and Armstrong, 2014: 40).

Most people love being asked to test out a new exhibit component. They feel like they are getting the inside scoop on the new exhibition and that their opinions are valued. Their input may even change the way the exhibition turns out. If they feel they really did have an influence, they may bring their friends: "See how that says 'to the left of the courthouse'? Originally it was going to say 'north of the courthouse,' but I told them that not everyone knew which way was north, so they changed it."

The third type of evaluation, summative evaluation, will be ongoing. The whole time the exhibition is open, keep using your visitors as evaluators. If you see someone who doesn't understand something, or if visitors ask questions about an object, find out how to make the label clearer. Then go rewrite it, print it, and mount it in the exhibit.

Mock-Up Testing

It is not practical to test your whole exhibition before you open. Try one exhibit case and one interactive component as test samples. An interactive component is something that visitors can manipulate, such as turning a knob, lifting a lid, or weaving yarn on a loom. You absolutely need to test your interactive components. Why? They are the easiest to get wrong.

You are going to pick at least one interactive component and one object case and make exhibit mock-ups to test on people. You want it to look rough and homemade. If you present visitors with a mock-up that looks like a finished product, "they don't want to hurt your feelings by being critical" (Serrell, 2015: 259). Make it out of cardboard, hand write the labels, and let people know that this is a test product you can easily change.

Learning from Experience: A museum I worked at obtained a child's record player and a stack of 45s that we could allow to get ruined. This was going to be an interactive component, especially planned for children who had never used a record player. I wrote up the instructions for how to use it, but I didn't bother to test it. After all, I'd used record players all my life. Imagine my embarrassment when on opening night the first child in the exhibit carefully followed the instructions and the record didn't play. What went wrong? I wrote, "Put the arm down on the edge of the record." I didn't say which edge. The child placed the arm on the inside edge next to the spindle. The very next day I reprinted it to say "outside edge of the record."

Image 6.1 This wooden model represents an actual Stegosaurus fossil. The labels would not be that large in comparison to the bones, but in this mock-up they needed to be big enough for visitors to read. Visitors easily understood the purpose of this mock-up. Project and photo by Gabrielle Ferrara.

The exhibit you are testing needs to be able to convey an idea without any other exhibition context around it, so select carefully. In the Exhibit Development course I taught at the University of Oklahoma, I give students a mock-up assignment. The instructions they receive will work well for your mock-up testing:

1. The interactive mock up can be made of cardboard and string, but it should work. The object case can be three-dimensional with actual objects (replicas) or can be a flat board with photos of the objects.

2. Write labels for the object case and the interactive. For the case, these should include a title, a main idea paragraph, and image and/or object labels. For the interactive, just write the instructions for using it. The labels should be easily changed. Handwritten labels are encouraged. Bring extra paper, markers, and tape.

3. Create a three-to-four-question visitor survey. The survey should determine whether visitors understand the concept of the panel or case.

4. Set them up in your museum or take them someplace where you can show them to the general public, such as a library or farmer's market. Explain that this is a mock-up of an exhibit your museum is planning and ask visitors to complete the survey.

5. Revise your labels, and perhaps your layout; then do the visitor surveys again.

6. Repeat step 5 as often as necessary until visitors understand the concept, or the exhibit is deemed a complete failure. Sometimes an idea for an exhibit just doesn't work and fails to convey the intended message. Failure is OK—learning from the visitor is the whole point of this exercise. (Hansen, Museum Exhibit Mock-Up, 2013)

The Survey for the Stegosaurus Mock-Up

We want to find out if this exhibit helped you answer these questions:

- Where is Stegosaurus found?

- What can you tell me about the Stegosaurus' plates?

- Can you tell me 4 facts about the Stegosaurus?

- If you could make any changes to this display, what changes would you make? (Ferrara, 2015)

Always remember that you are testing the label, not the visitor. It helps if you explain this to them up front. Their reaction is always right—it is the label text or the interactive set-up that is incorrect.

Beverly Serrell has some suggestions about how to question visitors. For object labels, you want to determine if visitors like it and understand it. More importantly, "Does their understanding coincide with (or at least not contradict) the stated communication objectives for the element?" (Serrell, 2015: 258) To test this, you might want to ask them to explain the exhibit case in their own words, so you'll know what it is they really understand.

For interactive components, you may want to do more observation than questioning. Can visitors figure out how and where to start the activity in 1.5 seconds or less? Can people follow the directions? Are the directions in three or fewer steps? Then ask them what it meant and whether it worked (Serrell, 2015: 258).

Examples

The Artist's Tools, created for University of Oklahoma Exhibit Development course.

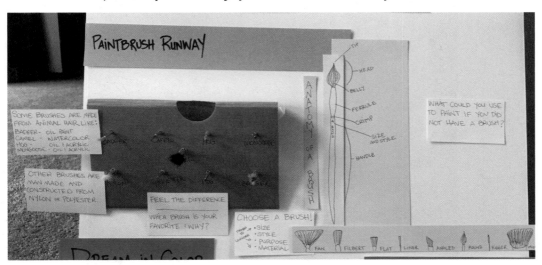

Image 6.2 Touchable panel explaining types of paintbrushes.

This exhibit, *Artists in Their Natural Habitat: An Insider's View of the Studio, the Inspiration and the Product* was intended to introduce visitors to the tools and working space of an artist. An entire section was mocked-up. Shown here are touchable "Tactile Panels" about paint and paintbrushes.

Questions for Test Participants:

Examine the Tactile Panel. Is it appealing?

Is it self-explanatory?

In a museum setting, would you feel that this exhibit is inviting?

Is this exhibit educational?

Please provide additional comments or questions.

    All of the testers seemed to enjoy the tactile engagement opportunities and needed no prompting to examine the various materials. One of the high school testers stated that the handling of objects was her favorite part. The paintbrush tops were by far the most handled; several commented that they did not know there were so many different styles of brush fibers or the names of the parts of a brush. The prompting questions gave an opportunity for our older testers to engage the elementary testers, as they discussed what type of paintbrush they preferred or where they would like to paint.

    The panel earned the expected amount of attention from testers and provoked questions about the actual exhibit, its space within the museum and when the exhibit would open. Next time, we will use flip tabs and other "hidden response options" for our testers who wish to try out their knowledge before seeing names and answers. (Wilson, Unpublished paper, 2015)

Field Jackets Are the Unsung Heroes of Paleontology, created for University of Oklahoma Exhibit Development course.

Image 6.3 Miniature field jackets represented the objects in this mock-up.

When paleontologists dig up dinosaur bones, they wrap them in plaster coverings called field jackets to keep them safe during transport. This exhibit was intended to educate the public about what these jackets are, how they are made, and why they are important.

Questions for Test Participants:

What is the exhibit about?

Did you learn anything?

Would you change anything?

If your friend asked about the exhibit, how would you explain a field jacket to them?

> The mock-up consisted of fabricated mini field jackets with labels. The introduction paragraph introduced what a field jacket is and its function. Then there were six steps, detailing the process of how a fossil goes from being in the ground to the lab.
>
> During the first round of visitor studies it was found that it was confusing to have six steps outlined, but only three examples. The steps were reorganized and written into four steps and another example was added. Now with four steps outlined and four examples another round of visitor studies was conducted. This round revealed that it may be confusing to not have paleontology explained.
>
> The next round of visitor surveys included suggestions about adding photographs from a real dig. This could better relate the field jacket to the visitor by providing a frame of reference. All of the comments were valuable towards making this label successful. (Kubier, Unpublished paper, 2015)

Traditional Wool Processing, created for the Rural Life Museum at the Tuckahoe Steam and Gas Association, Maryland.

Image 6.4 Panels explaining how wool was processed traditionally.

Every year, demonstrators brought spinning wheels to an event at the museum. Previous experience had taught the museum that many visitors were curious about how wool was processed but were too shy to ask the spinners. These two panels were mocked-up to help explain the process.

Bits of wool during various steps of the process were included on the board.

Will It Work?   **61**

Visitors were often observed touching them, and encouraging their companions to touch also. The most frequent comment was about the photo of the sheep who had escaped and not been sheared for seven years. At first, staff were concerned about whether this was distracting people from the point of the exhibit, but then realized that it was making the point it was intended to make—sheep need to be sheared for their own health.

Hands-On and Interactive Area, created for the Historical Society of Talbot County, Maryland.

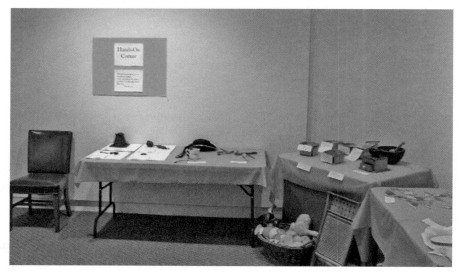

Image 6.5 Hands-on area mock-up.

Image 6.6 Hands-on area final version.

An entire hands-on area was mocked-up in this museum. In the "before" image, you can see that the whole layout is rough and looks temporary. It was left in that state for about six months. At the end of that time, permanent counters were built and signs made. During the testing phase, a decision was made about the color of the area as well.

Some interactive objects were removed because they were too confusing, and new ones were added. The instructions were modified on almost all of them. The chair was moved to face the area so that nonparticipants could watch the action, and it was replaced with one that had arms.

Worksheet 9

EXHIBIT WORKSHEET 9: MOCK-UPS

OBJECT TO BE MOCKED-UP _____

INTERACTIVE COMPONENT TO BE MOCKED-UP _____

WHO WILL MAKE THEM? _____

WHERE WILL THEY BE TESTED AND WHEN? _____

WHO WILL TEST IT AND ADMINISTER VISITOR SURVEYS? _____

LEARNING OBJECTIVE FOR THE OBJECT:

QUESTIONS TO ASK VISITORS:

1. _____

2. _____

3. _____

4. _____

LEARNING OBJECTIVE FOR THE INTERACTIVE COMPONENT:

QUESTIONS TO ASK VISITORS:

1. _____

2. _____

3. _____

4. _____

Conclusion

You have finally completed your preparation. You have learned a great deal about how to make quality exhibits that will engage your visitors and encourage them to support your museum.

The rest of this book will provide instructions on how to actually create exhibitions. We will cover building or modifying exhibit cases, mounting objects, lighting the room, and all those practical topics.

Congratulations on having done the work that provides a good basis for creating excellent exhibitions. Did you complete this work in the time you estimated when you created your timeline? You and your museum are on track to present your visitors with exhibitions that are polished and professional.

To-Do List

Select an object case to test.

Select an interactive component to test.

Fill out Exhibit Worksheet 9: Mock-Ups.

Make rough mock-ups.

Test the mock-ups. Revise, revise, and revise.

Sources

Falk, John H., and Lynn D. Dierking. *The Museum Experience Revisited*. Walnut Creek, CA: Left Coast Press, 2013.

Ferrara, Gabrielle. Unpublished paper for Exhibit Development course, University of Oklahoma, 2015.

Grewcock, Duncan. "Before, During, and After: Front-End, Formative, and Summative Evaluation." In *Manual of Museum Exhibitions Second Edition*. Edited by Barry Lord and Maria Piacente, 33–39. New York: Rowman & Littlefield, 2014.

Hansen, Beth. Exhibit Development Course Materials, Mock-Up, University of Oklahoma, 2013.

Kubier, Lauren. Unpublished paper for Exhibit Development course, University of Oklahoma, 2015.

McLean, Kathleen. *Planning for People in Museum Exhibitions*. Washington, DC: Association of Science-Technology Centers, 1993.

Serrell, Beverly. *Exhibit Labels, An Interpretive Approach, Second Edition*. New York: Rowman & Littlefield, 2015.

Soren, Barbara, and Jackie Armstrong. "Qualitative and Quantitation Audience Research." In *Manual of Museum Exhibitions, Second Edition*. Edited by Barry Lord and Maria Piacente, 40–54. New York: Rowman & Littlefield, 2014.

Wilson, Michelle S. Unpublished paper for Exhibit Development course, University of Oklahoma, 2015.

Chapter 7

How Will We Do It?

Now it is finally time to do it—time to build an exhibition. This chapter will include everything from A to Z, or rather from painting walls to setting lights. You will turn your floor plan or model into a reality.

Instructions for each step will be presented in the order you will carry them out. Your volunteer carpenters can get started on the temporary walls and exhibit cases months before your opening day, if you have a place to store them.

Your Local Community Theater

Before you get going, you may want to introduce yourself to your new best friend—your local amateur theater company. Whether this is a community theater or a high school drama department, you should call someone there and get to know them. They have windows, furniture, props, costumes, lights, and a variety of things that you might find useful. See if they are willing to give the museum a loan in exchange for a thank you on the donor panel and a mention in your museum newsletter.

Sources for Labor

If you are having trouble recruiting carpenters or handymen to build your exhibit, here are a few suggestions you might not have thought of:

* Youth groups as a community service project

* Boy Scout Eagle project or Girl Scout Gold project

* Habitat for Humanity volunteers during a down time when they don't have a house to build

* Any community group that is looking for a goodwill project

* Jail work release inmates (They are only eligible for work release when they have been on their best behavior, and they are often so delighted to be out of the jail they will do any task you ask. As a nonprofit, you are entitled to use their volunteer labor.)

Environmental Concerns

A word about preserving our environment—museum professional Kathleen McLean reminds us, "Long after the immediacy of their topics has faded and their designs have become passé, our exhibitions will still have an impact on people, whether piled in storage, disassembled for parts, languishing in a landfill, or burned in waste-to-energy plants" (McLean, 1993: 167).

For a small museum, saving money and being environmentally concerned are often the same. Using fewer materials, and reusing wherever possible, reduces both cost and waste. Creating cases, walls, and risers that can be used over and over will save time, money, and waste. Energy-efficient lights put out less heat and UV and are better for your artifacts.

Environmental graphic designer Yvonne Tang recommends considering the following factors:

* Be aware of resource and water management during every stage of a product's life cycle.
  ○ Reuse existing exhibition elements.
  ○ Specify materials made from recycled content (such as paper instead of vinyl for graphics).
* Employ efficient lighting technologies that use a fraction of the energy and generate less heat than traditional methods. (Tang, 2014: 337)

Ready, Set, Go

You will be very proud of what you have accomplished. I hope you hold a big opening party to celebrate. Now we get to have fun building an exhibition!

Walls and Hanging Systems

Your room layout and wall arrangement were designed in chapter 4. Now it is time to talk about how to use the permanent walls to create your display.

Drywall, or gypsum board, is the most common modern material for interior walls. It is a good surface for museum walls because it is "nailable, paintable, and repairable" (Maximea, 2014: 84–85). You can hang items on the walls, take them down, patch the walls, repaint, and hang new items.

An older building with real plaster walls will work best with a hanging system. Plaster is likely to develop large cracks when nails are put into it. It is harder than drywall and generally more difficult to work with. A hanging system will allow you to hang photos and label panels without putting nails into the actual walls.

If you are building a new wall, "a repeatedly nailable gallery wall is recommended to be constructed of 16 mm [⅝"] fire-rated gypsum wallboard over 19 mm [¾"] fire retardant treated plywood on studs. A supporting stud wall built to code under this double sheathing is generally strong enough to support the vast majority of art work or other items the museum might want to hang" (Maximea, 2014: 72).

Prep and Paint

Your first step will be to repair and repaint the walls. Many museums joke about their exhibition spaces becoming smaller and smaller because of the layers of paint. You would never add layer upon layer of paint in your house, but in your museum changing exhibition space, you can go ahead and paint over your old paint.

Paints that are low in *volatile organic compounds* (VOCs) are healthier for you and your artifacts. More and more paints are low VOC because of environmental regulations. Ask about it at your local hardware or paint store.

Flat paint works well in exhibit spaces. Semigloss may create glare on your walls, and eggshell gives an inconsistent finish. Naturally, you will want to consider your own situation—a dark room may benefit from the reflected light of a semigloss finish. Also consider how often you are going to repaint. Generally, I didn't worry about flat paint being harder to clean because I knew it would get repainted in a few months, but you may need the paint to last longer.

When you paint your walls, you will also want to paint your exhibit case bases. By painting the case the same color as the wall, the case will seem to disappear and the artifacts will stand out. On the other hand, you may want to make the cases a complimentary color to bring them to attention. Any decision is correct, just make sure you have thought about the colors you are using.

These are the steps you will want to take to get your walls ready for your next exhibition:

- Remove all nails, adhesives, and other items.

- Spread tarps on the floors.

- Patch holes and cracks.

- Prime the patches.

- Paint.

- Mark eye level on the walls.

Painting the exhibition walls can be a family activity. Children and grandchildren can come help, as well as teen groups who can receive community service hours for their help. Just make sure you have completely covered the floors with tarps. Canvas tarps with a rubber backing are the best because volunteers cannot track paint around as they can with a plastic sheet.

Temporary Wall Treatments

Sometimes you may want to temporarily add wallpaper, stencils, or fake windows. Instructions for this are in the period rooms section of this chapter.

Eye Level

Before we get into how to hang things on your walls, we will consider where to hang them. Museum visitors will appreciate labels and objects that are at a comfortable viewing height, so you need to think about where items will be placed.

Image 7.1 Visitors who are forced into uncomfortable positions will quickly move onto the next object or label, regardless of how interesting it is.

Visitor studies have shown that visitors will spend more time reading labels and looking at objects when they are comfortable. You will have people of all sizes at your museum, so how do you determine where to place items?

This chart will help you realize that everything people will want to look at closely should be no lower than 3 feet 5 inches and no higher than 5 feet 4 inches. Many museums and galleries use 58 inches (4 feet 10 inches) from the floor as their standard eye level. Large section heading signs can be higher because they will also be printed larger and are intended to be seen from a distance.

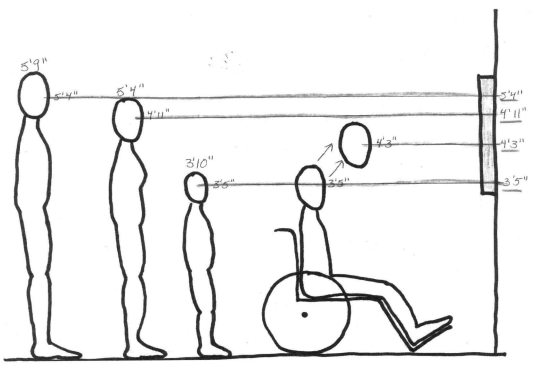

Image 7.2 These standard heights and eye levels are from the U.S. Department of Health and the Americans with Disabilities Act. The head height of people in wheelchairs can vary by up to ten inches.

For reading material, this gets a little more complicated. While holding their heads still, people can comfortable see 30 degrees above eye level and 40 degrees below.

Just about everyone over the age of forty needs bifocals, and this includes many of your museum visitors. Bifocals have the reading prescription at the bottom of the lens, so to read a label at eye level a bifocal wearer will have to tip back her/his head. Considering that the range of comfortable head movement is 30 degrees, compare the head positions of people with and without bifocals.

So, as you arrange your exhibition, your museum should keep in mind that:

- Standard eye level is 58 inches (4 feet 10 inches) from the floor

- Only large section headings and large objects can be placed above 5 feet 5 inches

- Labels and objects should be placed between 3 feet 5 inches and 5 feet 4 inches

- Hands-on objects can be placed at 3 feet 5 inches and below

Marking and Using Eye Level

After your walls are painted, create a temporary line at eye level—58 inches above the floor. This will help you keep all of the elements in your exhibition at appropriate heights. You can use a tape measure and a piece of chalk to draw a line around the walls of your exhibition space.

Carpenters use a chalk snap line to get a perfect straight line. It is an inexpensive tool and, if you will change exhibitions often, it is worth buying one. Make sure you only use blue chalk because it easily wipes off the wall. Other colors, such as red, orange, and yellow, are considered permanent.

Laser levels are becoming less and less expensive. You can use one to show you a perfectly straight and level line to draw. Or you can even find small ones that you can stick to the walls. There are apps you can download onto your phone to help you make a straight line.

If you want to center framed images and documents on the line, there is a simple method that will allow you to always get it perfect.

- Measure the height of the frame. Divide that in half. Example: 24 inches tall $\times$ ½ = 12 inches.

- Pull the hanging wire to its full height.

- Measure the distance from the top of the wire to the top of the frame. Example: 2 inches.

- Subtract this number from one-half of the frame height. This will be your distance above eye level. Example: 12 inches – 2 inches = 10 inches.

- Place a mark on the wall above eye level. That is where you will install the hanger. Example: 10 inches + 58 inches = 68 inches.

The frame is 24 inches tall.

Half of that is 12 inches.

The distance between the stretched wire and the top of the frame is 2 inches.

12 – 2 = 10 inches.

The hanger will be placed on the wall 10 inches above eye level.

58 + 10 = 68 inches.

The frame is centered on the eye-level line.

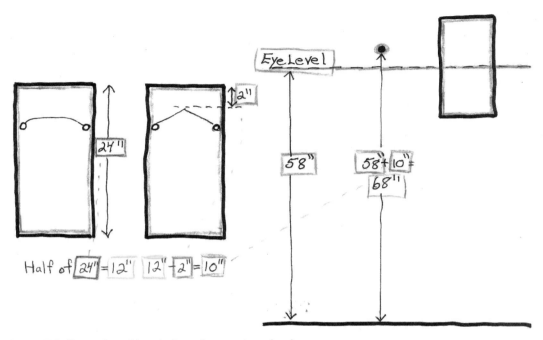

Image 7.3 Illustration of how to hang frames at eye level.

Applying Images and Labels Directly on the Walls

Many museums choose to apply images and labels directly to the walls. This allows you to use the entire space for your exhibition content.

Photos and documents in frames can be hung on the walls using a standard picture hanger. If the frame has much weight, use two hangers to provide the most support for the image—you don't want it to come crashing down. This requires carefully measuring to get both hangers at the exact same level.

There are a number of ways to attach labels and mounted copies of images to the walls. You will want to consider how long the items will be hung and how much they weigh.

If the exhibition is very short term, you might consider removable putty adhesives or temporary adhesive strips and hangers. Either of these products can be used to hold lightweight objects for weeks. The putty peels off easily and can even be reused. This is ideal for exhibitions that change often.

For an exhibition that will be up for months, you can use either adhesive Velcro or double-sided mounting tape. These will attach permanently and should only be used for copies of images and text labels. Each has its advantages and disadvantages.

The mounting tape should be permanent tape, and I prefer foam tape because the foam allows for minor variations in the surface of the wall. This cannot be repositioned—once you have stuck it to the wall it is stuck. It will permanantly stick to the object, too. You will remove a layer of paper when you pull it off, so only use it on labels and copies of images. When purchasing mounting tape, be sure to order large rolls from an art or office supply company. The cost for an entire exhibition is significantly less than buying the little rolls you can find at the drug store.

Removing mounting tape may mean pulling off a layer or two of paint from the wall. Or it may leave a sticky mess that must be scraped off and removed using chemicals such as Contractor's Solvent or Goo Gone. Either way, you will then have to patch and prime the wall.

Adhesive Velcro is also strong and permanent. Make sure you get a big roll of the industrial strength from an art or office supply company. There are a couple of options—you can get the standard width and cut it into pieces, or get the round dots. Labels generally require only a dot at each top corner, but larger images and section headings may need long strips. The adhesive Velcro cannot be removed from the backs of labels without taking off a layer of paper. Only use it on labels and copies of images or mats holding images.

When removed, Velcro will also stick to your walls. I have found it a little easier to remove than the foam tape when I use a putty knife to pry it off. You will still have to clean, patch, and prime. What I like best about Velcro is that I can move the position of the label or image. If I hang something crooked, I just pull apart the Velcro and adjust it. If I decide I want it a little lower, I can move it a bit.

There are more images on the website, so be sure to check it out.

Image 7.4 The large images and their labels are easy to read on the walls of this exhibition. Notice that the photos on the right are just a bit higher than the objects in the case. The images on the left are above the case, but they highlight objects in the case and do not have their own labels. Hennepin History Museum, Minnesota.

Panels on the Walls

Using panels allows you to get a lot of images on the wall with only a couple of nail holes. It also organizes the information so visitors can make sense of it. Exhibitions made with panels have a less cluttered look. There is a section in this chapter about how to make panels.

Image 7.5 The use of different colored panels makes it clear that each one is a separate topic. This exhibit used an alphabet theme. Historical Society of Talbot County, Maryland.

Hanging Rails and Systems

There are ways to hang exhibits without making any holes or sticky spots on the walls. Professional gallery hanging systems are expensive, but there are other choices. "Alternatives include hanging the objects from a wooden railing permanently affixed to the walls or from hooks screwed into the ceiling" (Dillenberg and Klein, 2012: 91). You can also consider map-hanging strips with cork. There are more images on the website.

Picture Rails

Sometimes the best technology is old technology. Houses with plaster walls frequently were built with picture rails on the walls. These wood ogee rails ran the length of the room a few inches from the ceiling. You could then use hooks to hang pictures on the wall without putting nails into the plaster.

You can still buy picture rails and the hooks designed to fit perfectly over them. This will allow you to change exhibitions without repairing your walls. Vintage photos of Victorian homes show that they used these rails to hang photos above each other, up to three tall on the wall.

Image 7.6 Large picture rails and hooks were used to hang a variety of framed artifacts and images around this organization's exhibition space. Washington Light Infantry Museum, South Carolina.

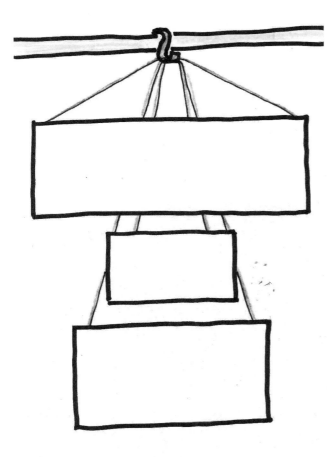

Image 7.7 A picture rail can hold multiple items on a single hook, as long as none of them are very heavy. Place the bottom item on the hook first, and hang the others on top of it.

Hanging Systems

Picture rails can also be used with hanging systems designed for them. These have hooks that go over the rails and rods that hang down the wall. Adjustable hooks can be slid up and down the rod to vary the height of the image. If your museum frequently changes art on the walls, a system like this can be a good investment. Utilizing wood picture rails will cost less than buying a specialized hanging system.

You can also buy a hanging system with its own type of rail if you will use it often and have the money to spend. A quick search on the Internet will reveal a myriad of systems. They usually have their own type of bar and hook and are not interchangeable with each other. A hanging system will cost considerably more than a wood picture rail, so you will have to consider the types of exhibitions you will mount and how often you will change them. Hanging systems are perfect for art galleries.

Map Hanging Strip

Map strips are handy for very lightweight items. Keep the weight restriction in mind for any place you decide to install these. Make sure you get the strips that can take hanging hooks. These will hold more weight, and look more professional, than using pushpins stuck into the cork. The hooks slide along the strip so you can adjust the placement on the wall. These strips are significantly cheaper than hanging systems.

Temporary Walls

Movable or temporary walls allow you to subdivide or reconfigure the space. They can be rearranged with every exhibition. Sometimes they may not all be used, which will require storage space for them. Walls that are relatively lightweight and small or can be folded or dismantled are the best choices. Visit the website for more images.

Folding Screens

Folding screens are easy to store and purchase. They can be made of wood, fabric, or bamboo. Screens that are in good shape have a professional appearance that will enhance your exhibition space.

Image 7.8 These screens block access to a stairway and convert an unusable corner into exhibit space. The exhibit panels are hung by monofilament (fishing line) from a nail at the top of each screen so that they can be easily changed. Trappe Rural Life Museum, Maryland.

Hollow Core Doors

Doors designed to be used inside houses are usually hollow inside. This makes them lightweight. Doors with real wood surfaces can be painted and patched, just like walls. Best of all, you can buy them inexpensively.

Doors can be given bases to hold them upright on their own. Alternatively, they can be hinged or hooked together to make long walls, or set up at angles like folding screens. They can be configured in many ways and are my favorite piece of exhibition furniture.

If you want to take them apart to store, line up the hinges very carefully so that any door will fit onto any other door when you use them for your next exhibit. Remove the pin from the hinge to separate the doors.

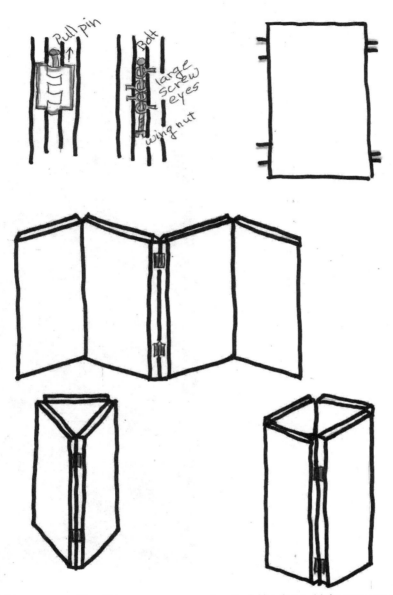

Image 7.9 You can use either hinges or screw eyes to attach the doors. Make sure you set up every door exactly the same so that all attachments line up to every other door. This shows some of the ways you can arrange them.

Image 7.10 A door with a heavy base is easy for visitors to walk around, and yet hard to tip over. This is very useful as an exhibition or section heading. Furniture sliders on the bottom corners allow a volunteer to move the door panels around the room easily, without damaging the floor. Historical Society of Talbot County, Maryland.

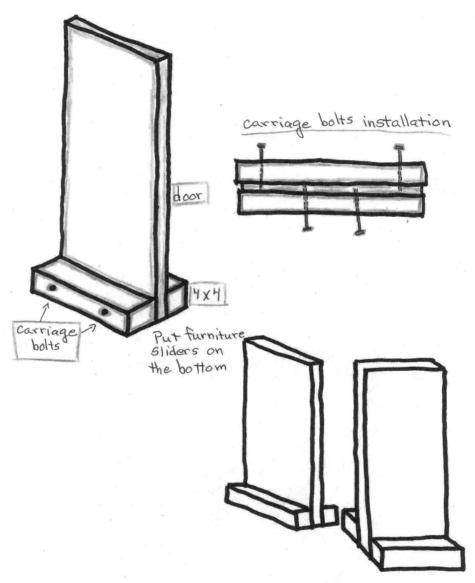

Image 7.11 Use carriage bolts or all-thread rods with washers and nuts to attach a 4 × 4 to each side of the bottom of a door. Put furniture sliders on the bottom to make the doors easy to move around the exhibition space. These temporary walls can be set up to create walls and corners.

Exhibit Cases

Exhibit cases are the most important piece of exhibition furniture in your museum. They can be easy to build and can last for decades. With a little thought, they can be flexible enough to work for any exhibition you want to create.

There are a few basic types of exhibit cases—floor cases and wall cases. Display cases from a store can be repurposed for a museum, but these were designed for retail and are usually too low for comfortable museum viewing. In a store, the clerk stands behind the case and talks to the customer, but in a museum you want artifacts close to the visitor's eye level. Retail cases can often be obtained for free when a store remodels or goes out of business, so many small museums use them. Later in this chapter, you will see how you can modify them.

Large museums often build custom cases for each exhibition. Make contact with someone at a large museum who can let you know when they have cases they can no longer use that they are willing to donate to your museum.

Floor Cases

You will be best served by making plain cases that are essentially cubes with removable plexiglass cube tops, called vitrines.

Image 7.12 The typical floor case is made of two cubes—a wood base and a clear top, called a vitrine. These two cases are the same size, but the vitrines are different heights. Also notice that the cases are painted the same color as the walls so that they will blend in and the artifacts will stand out. Hayward Area Historical Society, California.

Chapter 7

A volunteer at your museum can easily make the bases. The instructions are later in this section.

The tops, called vitrines, are made from the plexiglass or acrylic. You can make them, but I've never been satisfied with the results. It is very difficult to get even, square corners. You are better off purchasing the vitrines or getting them made by a local glass shop. This will probably be the most expensive part of your exhibition furniture.

To get the most versatility from your exhibition furniture, select a few basic sizes and shapes. Make just two sizes of bases—a square and a rectangular—and get vitrines that are low, mid-height, or tall. You can fill out a grid like this:

	Square	Rectangular
Low Vitrine		
Midheight Vitrine		
Tall Vitrine		

By making the effort to make sure your case bases of each size are exactly the same dimensions, you can switch the vitrines to suit a variety of artifacts.

Vitrines

Plexiglass or acrylic will work for the vitrine. It should be ¼-inch thick. If you want to try to make your own, there are many videos on the Internet that will show you how. Start with a small box and work up to a large case.

The vitrine maker will need to drill holes in the bottom for security screws to screw the vitrine into the top piece of the base. See the illustration in the section on bases.

Bases

The height of the base needs to accommodate comfortable viewing for standing adults, children, and people in wheelchairs. Check current ADA requirements for wheelchairs.

You will want to carefully select the materials you use to make the cube base. The exhibit cases must be chemically inert so they don't harm the artifacts inside. Many types of plywood and particleboard contain formaldehyde that will slowly off-gas over time. As museum expert Heather Maximea wrote in the *Manual of Museum Exhibitions*, "Many materials used in construction and finishing have the potential to off-gas chemicals that can cause deterioration to museum objects. . . . With 'green' initiatives, materials such as low VOC (volatile organic compounds) paints are now available that are safer for humans, the environment, and museum objects" (Maximea, 2014: 80). They are also becoming more and more standard. Ask at your local hardware or paint store.

Plywood bases are strong yet relatively light. Particleboard bases are very heavy, difficult to move around, and also contain more formaldehyde.

It may seem appealing to put trim on the cases, but resist that urge. You will want to frequently repaint these bases, and if they are plain you can just run a roller up each side and be done.

To build a case you will need:

- ½-inch plywood

- 2 × 2 lumber

- Wood screws

- Wood glue

- Furniture sliders

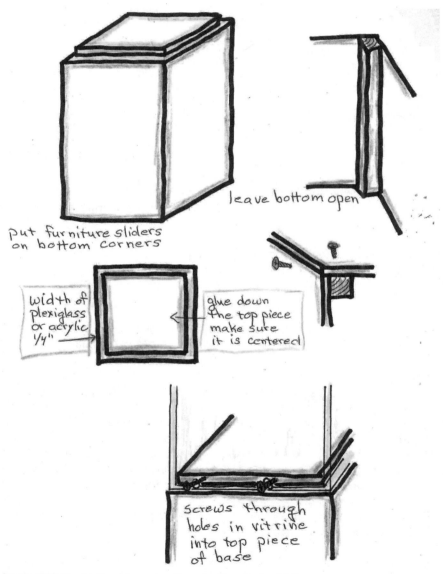

Image 7.13 Illustration of construction of a standard exhibit case.

Wall Cases

Cases that hang on the wall look very professional. Yet they are no harder to make than a standing floor case. They attach to the wall with a cleat.

If you make the base the same size as your rectangular floor case, you can switch the vitrines. You will want shallow ones for the wall cases.

Image 7.14 These items of ceremonial clothing are gathered into one wall case, along with a photo of them being worn. Indian Cultural Museum, Yosemite National Park, California.

Image 7.15 An empty wall case seen from the side.

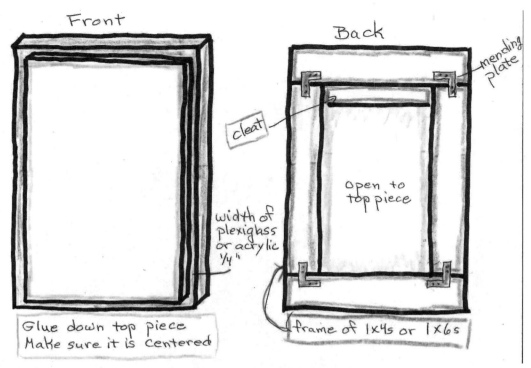

Front

Back

mending plate

cleat

open to top piece

width of plexiglass or acrylic ¼"

Glue down top piece
Make sure it is centered

frame of 1x4s or 1x6s

Image 7.16 This case starts with a rectangular frame. The top piece is centered on the frame, leaving a lip the same size as the width of the vitrine top.

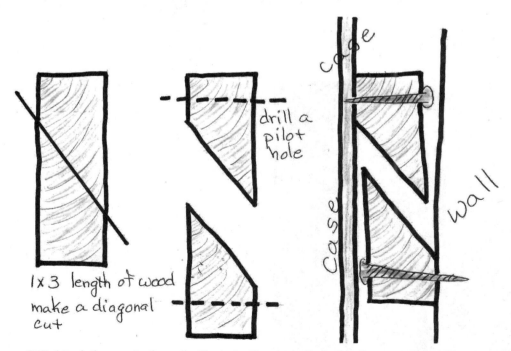

drill a pilot hole

case

case

wall

1x3 length of wood make a diagonal cut

Image 7.17 Attach the case to the wall with cleats. The cleat attached to the case will be left permanently and can be glued on. Drill a pilot hole into the other one and use a longer screw than shown in the drawing above. When you take the exhibition down, tape the wall cleat to the back of the case it came from, because they are all probably a little bit different. I find it helpful to write "Wall Side" on the correct side so the next time I go to use it I don't screw it onto the wall the wrong way. You can also make cleats out of foam core for mounting labels and images on matboard.

Wall Shelf Cases

For small objects that you want to highlight or to place near a photo or wall panel, these little shelf cases are ideal. There are more ideas about how to use them on the website.

Image 7.18 These shoes are perfectly displayed in a small wall shelf case. Historical Society of Talbot County, Maryland.

Image 7.19 Wall shelf cases are easy to build. You can use purchased shelf brackets or make your own. See image 7.17 for instructions for the cleat.

Retail Cases

The most frequently used case in small museums are retail counters. Retail counters have a few advantages—their shelves are usually glass, which allows light to pass through, and they sometimes have lights inside. Best of all, they can be found for free when stores update their look.

Display cases from retail stores have the problem of being too low. In a store, the staff stand behind the case and talk to the customer over the merchandise. In your museum, you want visitors to just look at the objects in the case, which should be closer to eye level. You will need to make sure you tilt items in the case at an easy reading level, and arrange objects so that each one is lit.

Image 7.20 The artifacts and photos on the lower shelves of these cases are nicely angled to make them easier to view. Washington Light Infantry Museum, South Carolina.

Image 7.21 No matter how well you arrange artifacts in a low retail counter case, they are still difficult for adult visitors to see clearly. Washington Light Infantry Museum, South Carolina.

Fortunately, the height issue can be resolved. This method was developed many years ago at the Adirondack Museum, Blue Mountain Lake, New York, and featured in the book *Help for the Small Museum* (Neal, 1987: 51). The idea is still as valid as the day that book was written.

To build a stand for your retail case, you will need:

- ½-inch plywood

- 2 × 3 lumber

- Wood screws

- Tape measure

Match the instructions to the drawing.

- Measure the existing case.
  - Find the vertical center of the glass.
  - Measure the distance from the center of the glass to the floor.
  - Measure the height of the toe kick at the bottom (see drawing).
  - Measure the outside of the case.
- You will want the center of the glass to be at a height of 58 inches.

    58 inches minus height of center = height of new stand

  Example: if the center of the glass is 24 inches

    58 – 24 = 34

  That number is the height of your new stand.
- Cut the plywood to the outside measurements of the case, and the height you just computed.
- Paint or laminate to match.
- Cut four pieces of 2 × 3 to the height of the new stand, minus the toe kick space at the bottom of the original case (see drawing).
- Put the stand together by installing a 2 × 3 into each corner and screwing the sides into them.
- Put furniture sliders on the bottom.
- Lift the case and place it in the stand so the bottom of the stand rests on the 2 × 3s.

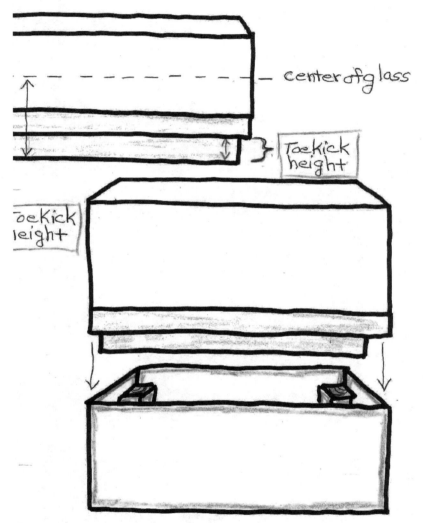

Image 7.22 It is easier than you might think to raise a retail case up to eye level.

Using Display Cases from Other Sources

There are a number of other sources for exhibition furniture. Architects use vitrines for models, gun display cases have large glass panels, and discount furniture stores sell shop-worn glass shelving units. Large frames can be used for flat artifacts, such as sheet music. Keep your eyes open and start to think of everything as potential exhibition furniture.

Image 7.23 A single trophy case with a built-in light makes a nice case for a small exhibit that changes topic seasonally or monthly. You can even create a wall of matching trophy cases. They can be hung at eye level, usually have glass shelves, may have internal lights, and even locks. The problem with these is that they are not very deep, and only thin objects can be used. You may be lucky enough to find a club or office that doesn't want its display case anymore. San Pablo Historical Society, California.

Barriers

It is important to place barriers of some sort between the visitor and objects. In general, if people can touch something, they will. You need to have something to indicate they should not touch. In a museum, even placing an object on a pedestal will create the impression that this is something special, and the public will generally respect that.

Unfortunately, theft is a problem in museums. Small objects not in cases should be tied down to the table with monofilament fishing line.

Stanchions

Stanchions used by banks and other businesses are easily available and have the advantage of being weighted at the bottom. They are expensive to purchase new, so ask around to see if some business is buying a new barrier system and is willing to take a tax deduction for donating their old one to you. You can also find used ones on online bidding websites.

But it is easier than you might think to create your own using lumber or stairway newel posts. Once the post is assembled, just drill a hole through the side. They look quite professional, especially when gold rope is looped through them. Instructions are below.

Image 7.24 Museum volunteers made these stanchions, used here to rope off a period room display in a large exhibition space. They are basically a post with a base on the bottom and a ball top. The label stands are described in the section on labels. Historical Society of Talbot County, Maryland.

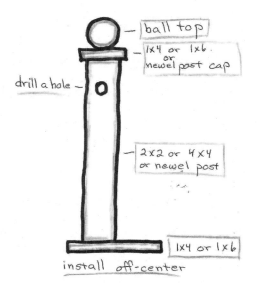

Image 7.25 When you make these stanchions, the post needs to be installed off-center on the base to allow visitors to walk by the rope barrier without tripping over the base. The larger side of the base will face into the exhibition. These stanchions can be made simply for a very low cost, or you can buy a stairway newel post, set it on a base, and drill a hole for the rope.

Risers

Just placing an object on a platform or riser sends a message to visitors that this item is special. Risers like this are usually already built and stored by theatrical companies. Your local community or school theater department probably has a number of them. Theaters are usually quite willing to loan or rent risers to your museum, especially if they are thanked in the label. Be sure to ask first, but they generally don't mind if you paint any item you borrow because they repaint them for every show anyway.

Risers can be built by your own museum volunteers. Instructions are shown later in this section.

Image 7.26 These mannequins were set on risers of various heights, borrowed from the local community theater. The risers help set off the clothes as displays and bring them closer to eye level. You can make these PVC mannequins yourself—see the section of this chapter on mannequins. Hayward Area Historical Society, California.

Image 7.27 If this chair were on the floor, visitors would probably sit on it. By placing it on a riser, it is brought to attention as an artifact. Additionally, visitors cannot walk right up to it. You may want to go one step further and either put a rope or ribbon across the seat or put a sign on the seat itself. New Orleans Collection, Louisiana.

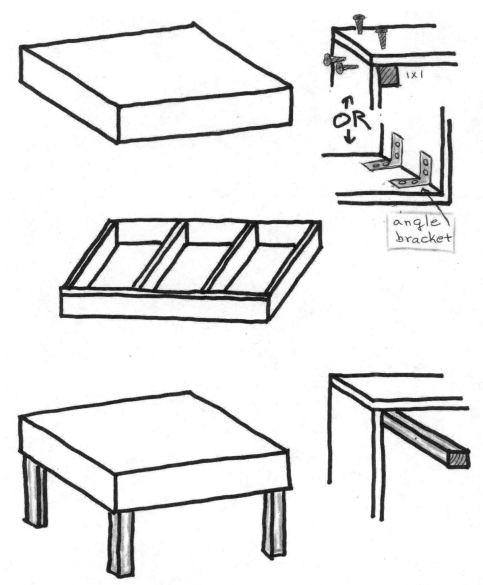

Image 7.28 The basic riser and platform are easy to construct. To make it a platform, install longer 2 × 2s in the corners to create legs.

Plexiglass Barriers

Sometimes you need some plexiglass so that visitors can see everything but cannot touch. Corner supports may be all you need. Please see the website for more ideas.

Image 7.29 The surface of this work table was constructed to act as the bottom of an exhibit case. Sheets of plexiglass or acrylic are supported at the corners. Screws at the bottom go directly into the worktable. There is no top. If you build a barrier like this, be sure to create an easy way to open it to dust the tools. Carver County Historical Society, Minnesota.

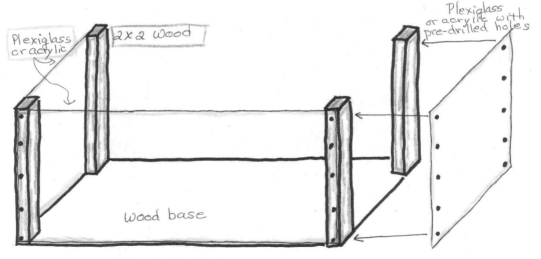

Image 7.30 Instructions for plexiglass barrier.

Doorways

If visitors cannot go all the way into a room, you will need a barrier. It is best to put the barrier inside the room, away from the door, so people can step inside a bit. This allows a much better view and allows the visitors to feel that they are in the room. Sections of fencing, garden gates, half of a dog crate, and a variety of other objects can be placed at a right angle to create a space to stand in a room. Tall dog gates work well as barriers but prevent visitors from stepping into the room. There are more images on our website.

For a barn or other outbuilding, a wire fence can be constructed a few feet inside the building. If it is three sided, it can provide a good-sized space for visitors to stand in. This allows the museum to leave the door open and both protect artifacts and prevent visitors from touching sharp implements when no staff is present.

Image 7.31 Visitors to Colonial Williamsburg can step into side rooms to get a good view of the furnishings. Think about how you can achieve the same goal using materials you can find at a hardware store, such as iron fence pieces set at a right angle. Colonial Williamsburg, Virginia.

Period Rooms

Creating a period room, or a section of a period room, is an effective way to help your visitors understand a time period. Exhibit cases with objects are lovely, but setting the objects in a room puts them in context.

Visitors may not have a mental image of what a home or clothing looked like during a specific time period. We can use terms such as *colonial, westward expansion,* and others, but what do they really mean? The era of Daniel Boone's West is different from the era of the Alamo's West. When we show rooms and clothing, people are able to recognize the look. It helps them know when events happened.

A period room doesn't have to be a complete room. Often, just roping off a corner of your exhibition space provides a setting to create a room. There are more images on our website.

Barrier and label stand construction are discussed in other sections of this chapter. Sadly, the barrier is necessary—a tin of Prince Albert tobacco was stolen from the Victorian room featured below. It was close enough to reach, so someone did. Keep small items out of reach, or tie them down with monofilament fishing line.

The labels can tell people about the time period, the room, the clothing, and specific objects in the room.

Image 7.32 Victorians loved wallpaper, but the museum didn't want to have to strip it off the walls at the end of this exhibition. So the wallpaper and border were stuck up onto the walls with double-stick tape at the top and bottom. There is no window behind the curtain. Historical Society of Talbot County, Maryland.

Image 7.33 Visitors are allowed to enter the room and walk around this desk, so a sheet of plexiglass protects the contents. It is attached at the front and sides with mirror clips. United States Postal Museum, Charleston, South Carolina.

Remember that your local theater company has walls, windows, and doorways that you can borrow. Since they repaint for every show, they probably won't mind if you paint the sets. Theaters also have fireplaces, chairs, curtains, and so on. As I've mentioned before, your community or school theater can be your best resource for exhibition building.

Mannequins

Clothing looks best when displayed on a mannequin. Modern mannequins will not work for antique clothes, especially clothing designed for waist-trimming corsets. In addition, you will have the problem of gender—how many male versus female mannequins do you need? Best to get something totally neutral.

All of the ideas here are for short-term display. Antique clothing should not be displayed on these types of mannequins long term for a variety of reasons.

PVC Pipe Mannequin

Museum director Jim DeMersman introduced me to mannequins made of pieces of PVC pipe (DeMersman, 2001). The beauty of these is that they can be put together in any size (adult or child), can have heads or not, are very easy to take apart and store when they are not needed, and are low cost. PVC pipe is a plastic that off-gasses, so you will only want to use these for short-term exhibitions.

Image 7.34 PVC mannequins were used for a variety of clothing, genders, and ages. The wedding dresses were stuffed with polyester fiberfill wrapped in muslin to create bustlines and torsos. Hayward Area Historical Society, California.

When putting clothes on these mannequins, there are a few tips that will make your job easier:

Image 7.35 Hayward Area Historical Society, California.

Bustlines: Some dresses just don't look right hanging straight in the front. Polyester batting wrapped in unbleached muslin makes a lovely stuffing. Put the dress onto the mannequin, and then add your bundle of batting.

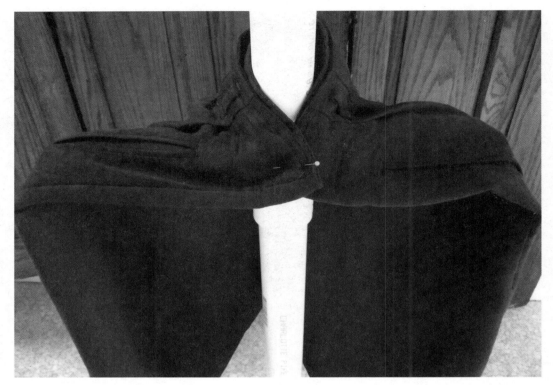

Image 7.36 The back of the mannequin shows the pants laying over the hip pieces and pinned together at the waist.

Pants: There is only one leg on the mannequin, so just wrap the pants around the waist of the mannequin. Use straight pins to tighten the waistband above the hip joint, and the pants will hang straight. Make sure the pins are fine point so they do not damage the clothing.

Build the PVC Pipe Mannequin

To make this type of mannequin, you will need:

- Wood base

- Metal floor flange

- Bushing to adapt flange to PVC pipe

- PVC pipe—1 inch or 1½ inch

- four-way joints (two per mannequin)

- three-way joints (one per mannequin)

- End caps (three per mannequin)

Instructions:

- Cut wood bases at least 1 foot square.

- Screw the floor flanges into the bases.

- Screw the bushings into the floor flanges.

- Cut the PVC pipe into the following lengths:

  (see drawings to indicate lengths needed for various sized mannequins)

  ½ foot (four per mannequin)

  1 foot

  1½ foot

  2 feet

  2½ feet

  3 feet

- Put the pieces together to make women, men, or children. DO NOT glue the pieces together. You will want to reuse the parts to make various mannequins over the years. A video of the process is on the website.

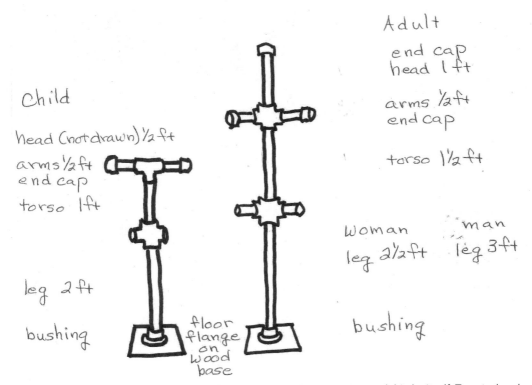

Image 7.37 For the child mannequin, the four-way cross joint creates enough hip by itself. To put a head on any mannequin, use a four-way joint at the shoulders and add a pipe and cap.

Image 7.38 Photo of PVC Mannequins.

Flexible Body Forms

These mannequins were purchased for a very reasonable price. They are called *flexible body forms*. The advantages of these is that the arms and legs are completely flexible so they can be posed in any position, they have no gender, and their waists are small enough to fit corsets. The disadvantage is that the rubber off-gasses. These should be used only for short-term exhibitions. You can make a flexible mannequin, but the cost of materials will almost equal the price of purchasing one. Instructions are on the website, if you want to try.

Sometimes you will need to stuff the clothing to round out the body shape. This is especially true for women's clothes designed with a bust. Polyester batting wrapped in unbleached muslin makes a lovely stuffing, as you can see in the Victorian clothing below.

Image 7.39 The flexible mannequins were used for World War II uniforms. The ability to pose them allowed one sailor to salute. Historical Society of Talbot County, Maryland.

Standard Mannequins

Of course, you can always choose to use typical store mannequins, if you get offered some for free. It is not recommended that you purchase these. They are too large for many historic clothing items; they are inflexible and difficult to dress, which increases the possibility of damage to clothing; and they have gender. All mannequins discussed here are made of plastics and off-gas, which can cause damage to clothing over the long term.

Interactive and Hands-On

Hands-on and interactive activities provide experiences for visitors other than looking. Technically, there is a difference—hands-on items can be picked up and handled, while interactive exhibit components do something, such as lighting up when you get the right answer. But for the sake of simplicity, they will be handled together in this chapter. Both interactives and hands-on require you to use items that are not in the collection, to encourage visitors to touch objects, and to consider how to get the activities ready for each new visitor.

In chapter 4, you were asked to think about whether you wanted hands-on activities or not. Now it is time to decide exactly what you will include in your exhibition.

Only include interactive activities when they are relevant. There is no need to add them just because you feel you ought to. They can be very helpful when explaining abstract ideas, especially in science or nature museums. For example, exhibit consultant Lisa Dillon Wright suggests that "challenging visitors to build a model of a bridge might be the best way to describe certain concepts of physics and engineering" (Wright, 2014: 287).

Hands-on activities can be very inexpensive. Just setting out a replica object for people to handle will satisfy the desire to touch. Although you've undoubtedly seen highly technical interactive exhibitions at large museums, you can keep your visitors engaged with simple objects and activities.

Keep in mind that visitors of all ages and abilities will want to participate in your interactives. "Controls for and operation of all interactives must be accessible and usable by all visitors" (Thompson and Thompson, 2014: 330). Hands-on objects can be placed at 3 feet 5 inches and below, and objects on tables or pedestals should be easily reached while in a wheelchair. If the wheelchair cannot roll under the table, there must be room for it to stop next to it.

Interactive components, which ask the visitor to do something, are the most important part of your exhibit to test. The instructions may seem clear to you, but they may not be to anyone else. Go back and look at the chapter on mock-ups (chapter 6) to remind yourself of some of the pitfalls of label writing. Whenever possible, an interactive should be tested with visitors before the exhibition opens to see if they understand how to use it and what it means. A cheap model can be made out of cardboard and tape, and the interactive can be easily changed if it does not work. Be open to continuing to change the instructions during the run of the exhibition.

Laminating the labels and instructions will help them last longer. Getting your own small laminator may be worthwhile. There are notes about laminating in the section on object labels.

People can experience the Internet anywhere. They came to your museum to see real things. "In the digital age, museum exhibitions . . . support face-to-face experiences with real and authentic objects, real works of art, and real people—a refreshing alternative and/or complement to a screen-mediated world" (Blankenberg, 2014: 165). There are situations in which digital technology is the perfect medium for explaining an idea in an exhibition. In those cases, it should absolutely be used. Digital technology changes quickly, so to find out what is currently popular either search the Internet or ask a teenager.

This section will provide just a few examples of the ways to provide visitors with tactile experiences. More are on our website, and thousands more can be found on the Internet.

Touch Objects

You need to convey two very clear ideas on the label for any object you will allow people to touch: (1) this can be touched, (2) this is not part of our museum's collection. You always want to make sure visitors understand that you take good care of the objects in the collection. People are more comfortable donating artifacts when they are assured they will be treated well.

It has happened that hands-on objects get broken or stolen. If it is an essential part of your exhibition, get more than one. Otherwise be prepared to remove the table and signage.

Touchable components engage more of visitors' senses and thus more of their brains. Nonaccessioned objects or modern-day replicas placed on "touching tables" are the most common and simplest type of hands-on materials. Raw materials like porcupine quills, buffalo or deer skins, and birch bark, provide excellent hands-on supplements to exhibits on Native American culture. Clearly identifying these as noncollection items helps visitors understand that the museum maintains appropriate standards for the care of its collection and does not allow accessioned objects to be handled. (Dillenburg and Klein, 2012: 81)

You may think that instructions to touch something would be the easiest exhibit labels to write. But museum label expert Beverly Serrell reported about a museum that tried several versions of a "please touch" label before they found that the most effect one had "please touch" written larger than the artifact name and also had a graphic of a hand reaching out (Serrell, 2015: 257).

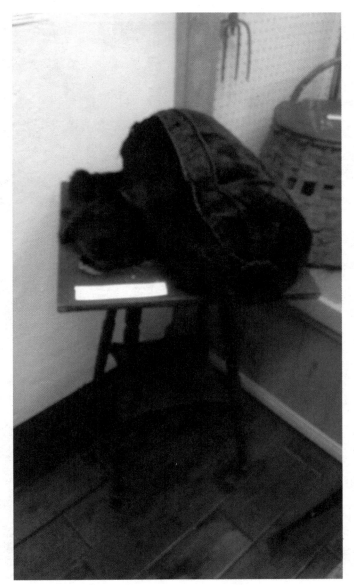

Image 7.40 An easy way to explain why beavers were hunted for their pelts is to let people feel a pelt. Many taxidermied animals contain formaldehyde, so a fur muff is a safer piece of fur to handle. It also provides an example of what the pelts were used for. The sign on the table tells visitors to touch the muff. Polk County Museum, Wisconsin.

Manipulate or Use Objects

People love to turn handles and use objects. "How does it work?" is a very common question when visitors see something they are not familiar with. Visitor studies experts John H. Falk and Lynn D. Dierking report, "Observation of visitors to museums confirm that . . . visitors are particularly attentive to the objects and to opportunities to interact" (Falk and Dierking, 2013: 113). Your museum can give people a unique opportunity to handle and manipulate something they couldn't see or use anyplace else.

Image 7.41 This coffee grinder is placed in front of a general store exhibit. Visitors can turn the handle and watch it in motion. Curator Shannon Dutra reported that "the 'Please Touch' signs have been in place since the museum opened to the public in the 1980s and they've been working well" (Dutra, personal communication, 2016). Campbell Historical Museum, California. Photo by Shannon Dutra.

Image 7.42 This manual typewriter was one of the most successful hands-on objects I ever put in a museum. Children loved it! We ended up keeping it in the permanent hands-on section of the museum. I will never forget the little girl who hit a key and said to her grandparent, "It prints instantly!" Just make sure you have paper and extra ribbon on hand and your volunteers know how to change them. Historical Society of Talbot County, Maryland.

Read Books or Other Materials

There are a variety of ways to set out a book for visitors to read. Make sure the label encourages people to read it or they may not be sure they are allowed to handle it. Scrapbooks provide additional information that visitors can choose to read or not. They can flip through and enjoy only the images and articles they want to see.

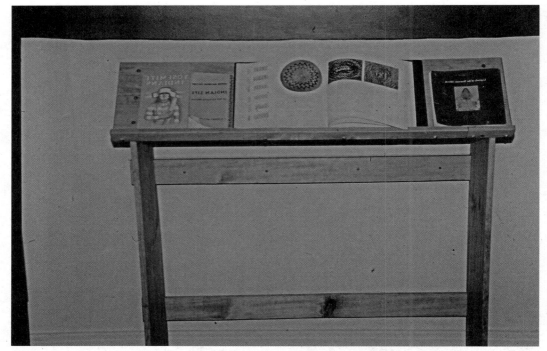

Image 7.43 This stand was made by a volunteer to hold multiple books at a comfortable reading level. It is a simple design, but it increased the number of visitors who looked through the books as compared to when they were on a low table. Indian Cultural Museum, Yosemite National Park, California.

Image 7.44 Visitors enjoy being able to flip through photos or documents at their own pace. These charts require an initial investment, but can be changed regularly to present new information to visitors with little effort. If using historic photos, place good quality copies on the chart so the originals do not get exposed to light or damaged. Polk County Museum, Wisconsin.

Test Knowledge

One of the most common hands-on activities is the flip panel. You've seen these at many museums—a question is posed on a little flap and you lift it to see the answer. Other ways to allow visitors to test their knowledge include quiz boards and puzzles.

It is important to remember that the visitors came to your museum to have fun, not to pass the SAT. You can quiz visitors on information in the exhibition, as long as the answers are easily found in nearby labels. The best flip panels pose questions that visitors themselves might ask, such as "Why did the Egyptians draw people sideways?" or "What is that tool used for?"

You read in chapter 5 about the tendency of people to block out negative words in sentences. If you display a true/false question with the statement "sharks eat people," they will remember that the quiz said sharks eat people, not that it was false. So use multiple choice or open-ended questions.

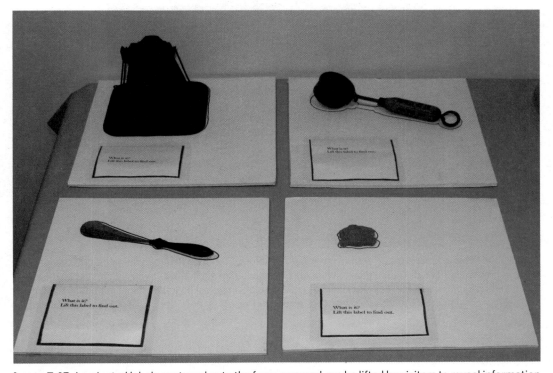

Image 7.45 Laminated labels are taped onto the foam core and can be lifted by visitors to reveal information underneath. They fall closed again for the next visitor. The objects are outlined so visitors will replace them on the correct board. Mock-up testing revealed that the top label needed to be outlined and the words "Lift this label to find out" written in order for visitors to use the exhibit as intended.

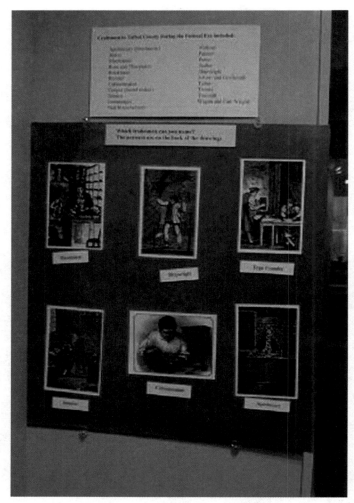

Image 7.46 This quiz was made with magnets. A thin piece of metal sheeting was hung on the wall with mirror hangers. Images of tradesmen at work and the names of their trades were laminated (with matte laminate), and magnetic tape was stuck to the backs. Visitors were asked to put the name under the correct image. The biggest problem with this was that it required resetting after each visitor. Historical Society of Talbot County, Maryland.

Experience Activities

Beyond being able to touch things, we can allow visitors to have experiences they wouldn't normally have. How often do people get to dress up in replica period clothing? Or try a craft? Living history farms and museums provide ample opportunities for visitors to engage in unique activities, but all museums can offer something.

Writing labels for activities can be tricky. You will probably have to try a few variations before you get instructions that work for most people. Beverly Serrell wrote that the labels must "invite, instruct and give clues about the nature of the interaction" (Serrell, 2015: 197). She suggests that the labels contain a "prompt for action, where to touch, what to notice, and a clue about the concept" (Serrell, 2015: 197).

Image 7.47 Dress-up is a favorite activity. If an exhibition features a historic time period, uniforms, or equipment, people love to try on replicas. In this case, there is clothing on tables on each side of a mirror, which was placed on a door panel. The mirror was a good visual clue to visitors that the clothes were there to be worn. There were also signs around the mirror telling people to try the clothes on. Historical Society of Talbot County, Maryland.

Image 7.48 Visitors were given an opportunity to try some needlework in this activity. Patterns were drawn onto the fabric, and thread and needles were set out. Most people who participated just took a few stitches. It took almost a year before a single design was finished and had to be replaced. Every morning before opening the volunteer made sure there were threaded needles. Rural Life Museum at the Tuckahoe Steam and Gas Association, Maryland.

Image 7.49 A traveling exhibition consisting only of framed photos was enlivened with an activity that involved packing a covered wagon for the trip out West. Everything was lightweight so that it could be lifted into the wagon. The sacks were labeled *flour, sugar*, etc., and stuffed with Styrofoam packing popcorn. The wagon was a wood frame with plastic PVC pipes bent across the top and covered with a sheet. There were intentionally too many things to fit in the wagon, so visitors had to make decisions about what to leave behind. Most people were good about unpacking the wagon when they were done. Hayward Area Historical Society, California.

Videos

Once upon a time, video was considered high technology in an exhibition. People still enjoy watching a short video clip. Remember that unless you provide comfy chairs, visitors will be standing up while watching, so keep it short.

Video can showcase traditional music, traditional crafts, and interviews with people who were involved in events. It can explain a process better than any still photos. For example, an exhibition about a community built around a steam sawmill was enhanced by video of a similar sawmill in action, filmed by a volunteer on their phone or tablet.

If you are using a DVD, you can set it to repeat all day. Just remember that your front desk volunteers will hear it over and over during their shift. A good solution is to have a loop of many songs or short videos. One museum used a two-hour video of old TV commercials for toys during a toy exhibition. Each commercial was only thirty seconds long, so visitors could walk away after only a minute or two. Volunteers didn't hear a repeat commercial for two hours.

Computer touch screens can allow visitors to touch to start a video when they are ready, and even to select which video they want to see.

Computers and TVs are one reason it is important to know where your electrical outlets are located when making your model of your exhibition space. You want to be able to plug into a wall behind the screen and have a clear viewing space in front of it. Chairs or benches encourage visitors to watch the video.

Image 7.50 This museum installed a permanent mount for the TV. If it was not needed for a specific exhibition, the arm was easily detached. The VCR player and controls were in the office manager's office on the other side of the wall. Hayward Area Historical Society, California.

Image 7.51 This exhibition utilized tablet computers on black metal tablet stands. "These tablet stands are built in such a way that a tablet can fit comfortably inside and visitors do not have access to the power or volume buttons" (Dutra, 2016). With touch screen tablets, presentations can be created that allow visitors to select topics they want to know more about. Campbell Historical Museum, California. Photo by Shannon Dutra.

Photo Display

Photographs are a very important part of any exhibition. We often take objects out of context and put them in cases when we create exhibitions. Photos show the objects in their original place, being put to their original use.

Photos can also show things too large to put in your exhibition, such as homes and big equipment. They provide invaluable context to your exhibition.

Original photos can be framed or matted. If you have glass in the frame, keep the image from touching the glass by using spacers, as described below.

If you are using the photo in an area with bright lights, or if it will be on display for a long time, consider using a copy.

Scanning or photographing the photo can give you very good copies. Then these copies can be mounted just like text labels. See the section on label production for instructions on how to mount copies of photos.

Frames

With a photo from your collection, you want to keep the image separated from the glass at the front of the frame, as well as the frame backing. You've probably seen a photo that has been in its frame for years and has attached itself to the glass. To prevent this, cut little pieces of matboard and stack them to the correct height to act as spacers between the glass and the image. Put a little stack at each corner of the frame.

Wood and most paper (which is made from wood) contain acid. This can damage photos over time. Acid-free papers and matboards are available at most art supply stores and should be used in photo frames and mats. If you can't use acid-free matboard for some reason (such as if you are using an antique frame), place a piece of acid-free paper between the photo and the back of the frame.

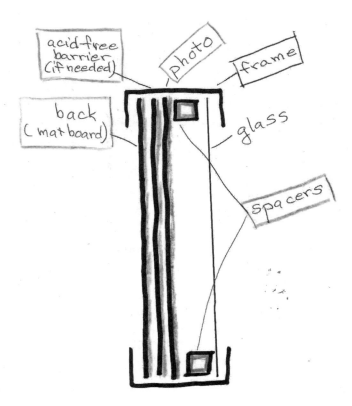

Image 7.52 This illustrates the process of framing a photo in the museum's collection.

Mats

Photo mats in standard sizes are available at most craft supply stores. Make sure to get acid-free mats.

Some mats will come with backs, possibly hinged to the front. If not, it is easy to cut a back to fit with a box cutter. Detailed instructions for cutting matboard are in the section on labels.

Supplies you will need:

- Acid-free mats

- Acid-free backs

- Archival corner mounts

- Photo tape or linen tape (linen is stronger)

Matting a photo:

- Attach the back to the front with photo tape or linen tape, if necessary. Do this by creating a hinge from the front to the back at the top.

- Center the photo in the opening on the front. Hold it in place with a small piece of photo tape.

- On the reverse side of the front, place acid-free corner mounts on each corner of the photo.

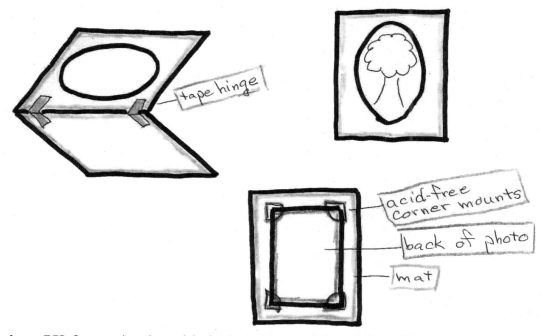

Image 7.53 Once you have learned the few basic steps to matting photos, it will be easy to do.

Labels for Objects

Labels identify objects and images for the visitor and make your collection of artifacts into an interesting exhibition. You thought about what your object labels would say in chapter 5. Hopefully you wrote some engaging and short labels. Now it is time to print and mount them. This section will focus on object labels. Headings and Section labels are in their own section.

Labels and copies of images are best displayed when mounted onto a flat, stiff surface. They can then be used for object labels, or used in wall panels. Making each label and image separately will save you time and money.

Chapter 5 explained why font type and size are important. As a reminder, most experts agree that the smallest point size that should be used is eighteen points (Tang, 2014: 315).

Beverly Serrell wrote:

> For most people, 18 points is the minimum size of body copy type for caption labels that is comfortably legible at twenty inches away, from a standing position, with good lighting, using dark type on a well-contrasted, light background. (Serrell, 2015: 275)

You will want to consider the size and shape of the label. How will it fit into the exhibit case or within the layout on the wall? Although you are using 8 ½ × 11 paper, your labels can all be different sizes. You will want to consider:

- Horizontal versus vertical

- Width

- Height

Sometimes it is best to print them all out and lay them in the exhibit case or tack them onto the wall to see how they look before you go to the trouble of mounting them.

You may want to include an image on the label. Scan the image into your computer and insert it into your text document for best results. An image can attract attention and make the label more enticing to read. Use images sparingly—if you put them into every label then they are no longer special.

An image on the label can enlarge an object too small to see clearly or show the back side of an object. Images are especially valuable for areas with multiple artifacts, such as tools, to help visitors identify the various objects. I also like to use them for artifacts many people are not familiar with. Many museums hang horse tack on a hook on the wall, but modern city dwellers have no idea how a plow harness is actually hooked up to a horse.

Image 7.54 Enlarged images of the designs on these coins were printed into the label, with space left above the images for the actual coins. Washington Light Infantry Museum, South Carolina.

Often workbenches have a number of tools that visitors are unfamiliar with. It is helpful to include a photo or drawing of each one with a description. Another solution is to put numbers in the case next to each tool and list their names in order on the label.

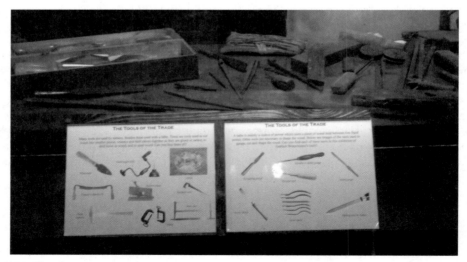

Image 7.55 The illustrations on this label make it easy for visitors to identify the various tools spread out across the workbench. Whenever possible, add photos or drawings of people using the equipment to help visitors understand what it is. Carver County Historical Society, Minnesota.

Make the Basic Label

To mount your labels and images, you will need the following supplies:

- Printed labels and photocopied images

- Double-sided adhesive sheets or spray glue and disposable gloves

- Matboard

- Cutting mat

- Box cutter with lots of extra blades or a strong paper cutter

- Straight edge—preferably a T-square

  This process requires careful attention, but after a while you will master it.

- Using either the double-sided adhesive paper or the spray mount, attach the labels to the matboard.
    - If you use spray mount, be sure to wear the disposable gloves and spray it outside the building.
    - You can place the labels on the matboard anywhere. They do not have to be straight at this point. You will cut them out later.
- Use your T-square and box cutter to cut out the labels.
    - Line up the edge of the T-square with the label paper, not the matboard.
    - If you have a clear T-square, you can use marks on the ruler to set the margin (the space you leave around the text).
    - After the first cut, use the T to make the other cuts.

Labels on Walls

If you have chosen to mount your exhibit components directly onto the walls, see the section on walls for advice on eye level and how to attach labels. You will want to consider how long the exhibition will be up before you decide to use removable adhesives or mounting tape.

Image 7.56 The placement of the label on the wall between the two portraits made it easy to find. It is printed on a light-colored paper that blends in with the wall to help the text stand out. Historical Society of Talbot County, Maryland.

Labels in Cases

Labels that are displayed with objects should be installed at an angle so that they are easy to read. The same rules apply as when placing objects in cases—human heads tilt comfortably only 30 degrees, and our eyes follow a line of sight 30 degrees above and 40 degrees below eye level.

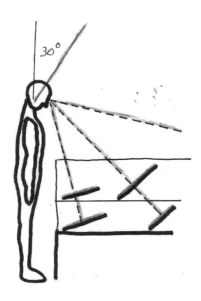

Image 7.57 Tilting the labels on display or in a case makes them easier for visitors to see.

There are two basic ways to angle the labels—use purchased stands or add a support to the back of the label using materials you already have on hand.

You can leave extra matboard at the top and fold it over to make a tent. To get a clean fold, score the fold by lightly cutting with the box cutter. The longer the piece of matboard is behind the label, the more upright the angle will be. You can always trim some off to make the label lean back more.

Alternatively, you can cut out an additional small square of matboard to be used as a stand. The extra piece is folded in half and glued onto the bottom back of the label. The square piece can be folded diagonally or straight across. The angle can be adjusted by the placement of the extra piece on the back.

Image 7.58 The backs of these labels show that each is supported differently. The two at left are on stands, and the two at the right have extra pieces added. The second-to-left stand was laid on its back to get a lower angle. The two on the right can be adjusted by how much you bend the matboard.

Even if you use stands, you will want to mount your labels onto matboard. It will make them stand up stiffly and will not allow light to shine through them. Both of these will make the labels easier to read.

Acrylic stands come in many sizes, from 3 × 5 to 8½ × 11. Most are designed to have a piece of paper slipped inside, but that will create glare. You will create the best label by attaching it to the front of the stand. Velcro dots are a good way to attach labels, and you can reuse the dots on the stand for many exhibitions.

Wire bookstands come in fixed and adjustable varieties. They will save you the need for adhesives. You can also find acrylic plate stands that will hold labels very nicely.

Labels Outside of Cases

Sometimes you just don't have room in the case for the labels. In that situation, you can number the artifacts and create a label with corresponding numbers, then put the label outside the case. This is not ideal. Visitors are much less likely to read the labels when they have to match up the numbers.

Image 7.59 Light green numbers mark the objects in this case, and a label is on the wall outside at the right. The numbers were created by printing a sheet of numbers on colored paper, mounting the paper on a piece of foam core, and cutting out each little square. You will want to save them to use again rather make new ones. Historical Society of Talbot County, Maryland.

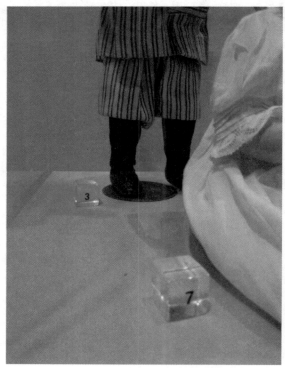

Image 7.60 Purchased plastic cubes and press-on numbers can also be used to identify objects in cases. Philadelphia History Museum, Pennsylvania.

Stands for Labels

Sometimes you need a label to stand in the middle of the room or in front of an object. Stands are fairly easy to make. You can stain the wood or paint it basic white. You want the label to be the focus, not the stand.

Image 7.61 Four triangles at the base make this stand very sturdy. A sketch is below. Historical Society of Talbot County, Maryland.

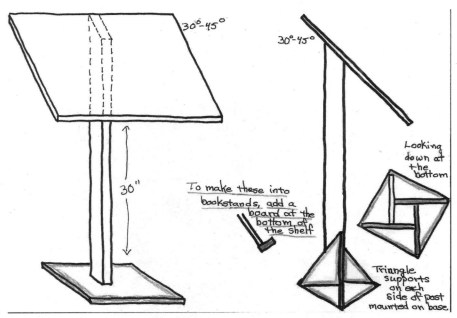

Image 7.62 Two similar stand designs are shown here. To make them into book stands, simply add a lip at the bottom.

Section Headings and Titles

You will need some labels and signs that are larger than the object labels. These include the main text for each section, the headings, a donor recognition sign, and the exhibition title.

These will be mounted the same way as the object labels. Please see the instructions in that section for how to mount them.

Naturally the font sizes will also be larger. The chart below was designed for students creating a science project display, but it is valid for a museum exhibition.

Table 7.1 Suggestions for a Typical Science Project Display Board

Item	Font Size (points)	Comments
Title	100+	You want your title to be visible from across a room!
Headings	36+	Should be easily readable from five feet away by someone just walking by.
Main Body Text	24–30	This is a comfortable text size for someone who comes closer to read more.
Objects/ Captions	18–20	People will be looking closely at the image or object.
Donor/Loaner Credit	16	This can be smaller than the standard font because it is not part of the story you are telling. People who really want to know who the donor is will read the credit line.

BASED ON: HTTP://WWW.SCIENCEBUDDIES.ORG/SCIENCE-FAIR-PROJECTS/PROJECT_DISPLAY_BOARD_FONTS.SHTML.

Section Main Body Text Labels

At the start of each section, you will want a label that gives the visitor general information about the topic for that section. This will be printed in a larger font to make it clear that this is the main label. Beverly Serrell suggests that "for introductory copy, group labels, or texts that will normally be read at a distance of greater than eighteen inches, the type size should be 28 to 48 points, depending on the conditions of lighting, space, color, and typeface and weight" (Serrell, 2015: 275). A point size of thirty points is recommended.

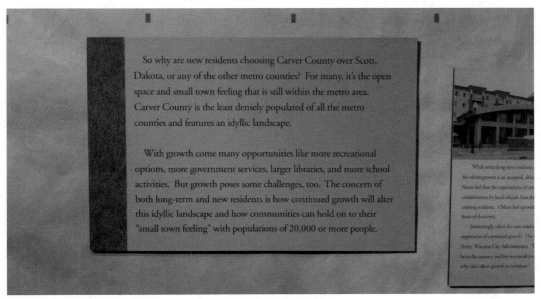

Image 7.63 The text font point size on the section main text is larger than on the image label at the right. The main text also has a colored band on the side to distinguish it. These can easily be printed and mounted at your own museum. Carver County Historical Society, Minnesota.

Depending on how you decided to install your exhibition, the main body labels may either be on a panel or installed on the wall. Sometimes they may even be in an exhibit case.

Headings

The section headings should be printed at thirty-six points. If you can print on 11 × 17 paper, they can be printed in one sheet. If you cannot print that large, you will have to decide whether to print multiple sheets of paper and mount them on the same matboard or to have them printed at a local print shop or office supply store. You can see a printed heading in the section on wall panels. Good calligraphy is an alternative, if you have someone who can volunteer to write signage for you.

Image 7.64 It is easy for the visitor to identify the subject of this exhibit case. The Section heading is in a large font point size and is very visible. Polk County Museum, Wisconsin.

Donor Panels

There were probably many people who contributed to the building of the exhibition. Volunteers who worked on the project, people who loaned artifacts, locals who provided information, and any organization or company that provided or loaned materials need to be thanked. Many museums create a donor panel near the entrance to the museum or exhibition.

The point size of the font will depend on how many people and organizations you need to list. The list can be adjusted to fit onto one 11 × 17 or 8½ × 14 piece of paper.

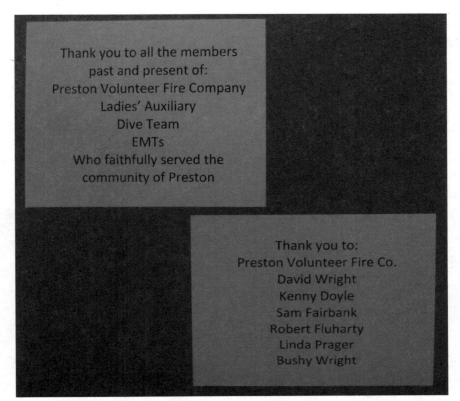

Image 7.65 Two thank-you lists were created for this exhibit—one for helping with content and one for loaning objects. These were printed on 8 ½ × 11 paper, mounted onto a half-sheet of matboard. Preston Historical Society, Maryland.

Image 7.66 Donors enjoy giving money for a specific purpose. This plaque recognizes funds for a pasture gate. Because it is outside, the museum had it engraved in metal, which is a nice touch. Similar wording can be used on a mounted paper label in an interior space. Greenbank Mills & Philips Farm, Delaware.

Exhibition Title

The font size for the title of your exhibition should be at least one hundred points. You want people to see it from across the room or from the front entrance of your building. This title entices people to come into the exhibition and see what it is about.

Titles can be printed on 11 × 17 paper, but you may not find that to be large enough. You may find a local company that is willing to give you a discount in exchange for a thank you on the donor panel. If you can't afford to get them printed, you can find someone who can do calligraphy, or use press-on vinyl lettering.

Image 7.67 The exhibition title faces the visitors entering this exhibit. The graphics introduce the visitor to the alphabet theme of the display. This was created on the museum's computer and printed out by a local printer. Historical Society of Talbot County, Maryland.

Image 7.68 An 11 × 17 paper printed on the museum's own computer created this exhibit title. The software allows a frame around the text, which helps the title stand out. Preston Historical Society, Maryland.

Wall Panel Production

Museums may choose to create each exhibition section in a single panel, rather than mounting each photo and label to the wall. This saves wear and tear on the walls and the volunteers, because an entire section creates only two nail holes rather than many sticky spots.

Wall panels organize your photos and text into sections. It becomes very clear where a section begins and ends—the section is on a panel. Sometimes it is necessary to use more than one panel per section, but they can be made the same color.

The panels can be designed on a computer and sent out to be printed. These panels certainly look professional. But I am going to recommend that you print each label and image, then mount them onto a matboard yourself.

Why should you print each label separately? Because as your exhibition is seen by the public, either they or you will find mistakes. There is nothing worse than purchasing a beautiful, professionally printed exhibit panel and discovering on opening night that someone's name is spelled wrong (except finding out how much it was going to cost to get that panel professionally reprinted—that was worse). I have seen that happen at two different museums, and in both cases multiple people had proofread everything.

Another reason for printing your labels and images separately is that you can print everything out at your own museum. Most of the images and text labels shown in the examples here are on 8½ × 11 paper. Some go up to 11 × 17 size. They were all created using software that came on the computer.

Layout

Whether you print in-house or send it out to be printed professionally, your panel should follow this basic layout:

Headline

100 point font

Main Text:

Basic Concept of this section

36 point font

Secondary Text: More information for people who were intrigued by the main text.   30 point font

Image or Object Label Text: Tell what the image or object is   18 point font

and who donated it   16 point font

Image or Object Label Text: Tell what the image or object is   18 point font

and who donated it   16 point font

Image or Object Label Text: Tell what the image or object is   18 point font

and who donated it   16 point font

Image 7.69 Panel layout suggestion.

Start by creating a plan for laying out your panel. Whether you do it on your computer or use a mock-up, you want to arrange your labels and images so that they can be seen in a logical order and look appealing.

Produced In-House

Not only does producing your own panels give you flexibility to make changes, it will save you money. Every element can be printed out on your own computer. No image on the panels shown here is larger than 11 × 17. In fact, many are 8 × 10 or less.

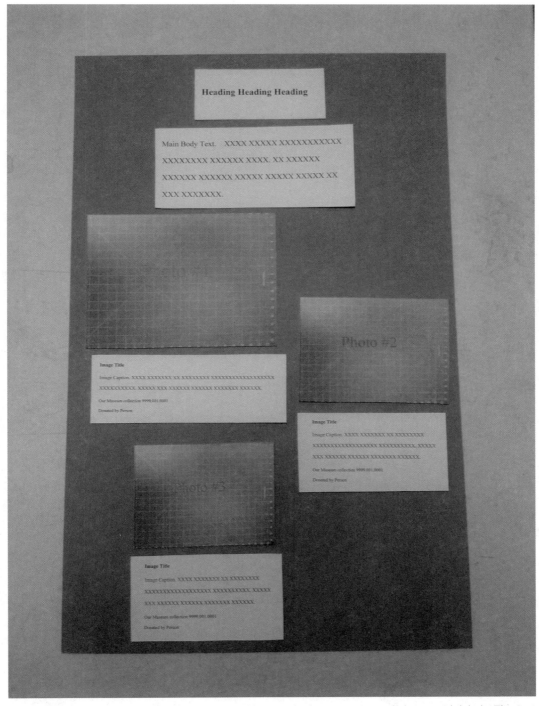

Image 7.70 This sample panel shows the typical layout of title, main text, and photos with labels. This just uses gray boxes and nonsense text for illustrative purposes. You can see how the text is largest on the title and smallest on the photo labels. If there is one photo that is the most important, you can make it bigger than the others.

You can re-create the look of a professionally printed panel by printing the labels on paper the same color as the matboard, or by creating a colored background in your word-processing program.

I learned this techique from museum director Glen Uminowicz, and I've used it ever since. The first time you use this system, you will need to create panel holders. Then you can reuse them for many years. The holders are simple to make; instructions are in this section.

Make the Panel Holders

You will use a piece of matboard as your panel front. Large matboard pieces are 32 × 40, so you will make the holder a little smaller. You can also make half-sized holders for those times you will need a small panel.

To make the panel holder, the supplies you need are:

- A piece of hardboard or foam core cut to a little smaller than 32 × 40 (31¾ × 39¾)

- Four art canvas stretcher bars: 2 at 20 inches and 2 at 30 inches

- Very strong glue (such as Gorilla Glue)

- Disposable gloves

There are just a few easy steps to follow:

- Put together the canvas stretcher bars.

- Measure carefully where you will want to attach the canvas stretcher bars. Make absolutely sure that they are completely parallel to the top so they will hang straight. If you are making multiple panels, make the stretchers the same distance from the top on all of them so your measurements for nail placement will be the same.

- Glue the stretcher to the back of the board. Be sure to wear gloves when working with the glue.

Image 7.71 To make sure the stretcher/hanger is exactly centered (left to right) and straight on the board, make very careful measurements before you glue it down. Make the measurement from the top the same on all of them.

To hang these, you will simply put two nails into the wall for the canvas stretcher bars to hang on. That's it. When the exhibition is over, you take it off the nails, remove the matboard with the current panel, and use it again.

Making the actual panels requires a few steps, but none of them are hard. It is a process that volunteers and community members can get involved in. You will need to mount each heading, main text, photo, and label. Then you put it all together on the matboard to make a panel.

The first step is to mount the text and images in the same manner as you did for object labels. See the instructions in that section.

Image 7.72 A 4-H member is working on a panel for an exhibition about her community. The labels have not been printed yet, but she is finding the best arrangement for the images. An orange paper at left is a space holder. Historical Society of Talbot County, Maryland.

To create a panel, you will need the following supplies:

- Mounted titles, main text, images, and labels

- Matboard

- T-square ruler

- Adhesive—Velcro or foam double-stick tape

Putting all the pieces together is easy:

- Lay all the mounted labels and images on the matboard. Play around with them until you get an arrangement that looks appealing and helps tell the story of the exhibition.

- One at a time, use a T-square to get the item straight on the board. Use Velcro or foam double-stick tape to attach it to the matboard. Velcro has an advantage in that you can move the item around a bit after you have placed it. The foam tape is permanent from the first time you put it down.

- After you have made the panel, attach it to the holder with either Velcro pieces or foam tape. I prefer the Velcro because I can leave them on the holder and use them again. They are good for many exhibitions before they have to be replaced.

Professionally Printed

Having your panels printed by a shop certainly adds to the professional appearance of your exhibitions. Your museum will not be able to make corrections over time, so if you want to do this, make a mock-up and leave it up for a while. You want to find your errors before you send it to the printer.

I recommend doing your own panels so that you can continue to incorporate visitor feedback. A permanent exhibit in a museum I worked at had been up for years before a visitor told us we had misused the terms *British* and *English*. Because we had printed it ourselves, I was able to print a corrected label and have it mounted and installed by the next day.

Object Display and Mounting

This is where you get to pull the artifacts out of storage and put them on display. Everything else you've done and will do is centered around exhibiting the objects and images.

Naturally, you want to protect your artifacts as much as possible. Your exhibition space should have as constant a temperature and humidity level as you can achieve. You will set the light levels so they are not exposing the artifacts to too much UV light. Ultraviolet, or UV, rays are the portion of the light spectrum that causes the most harm to artifacts. It is UV light that fades fabrics and photos. Now you need to protect your artifacts by the way you set them out for display. As exhibit developer Erich Zuern wrote, the goal is "presenting objects in a museum exhibition in an aesthetically pleasing manner that also supports the preservation of the artifact, work of art, or specimen" (Zuern, 2014: 366).

All museums also need to consider how the exhibit will look from the visitor's point of view. You will want to place artifacts in a way that will allow visitors to see them easily and completely. This section has a few suggestions and photos, but there are more on our website.

Large museums have a preparator who will custom make stands and holders for each object on display. You will probably be your own preparator, so this chapter will explain everything.

Prepare Your Exhibit Cases

You should have painted the cases while you were painting the walls of the room. At that time, you considered whether to paint the interior white. There are two advantages to white—one is that your objects will stand out, and the other is that you won't have to repaint with each exhibit change. This will reduce the exposure of your artifacts to paint fumes (and reduce your workload).

Some museums cover the interiors of the cases with unbleached muslin fabric. Unbleached is important because you don't want bleach fumes in the case with the artifacts. If you chose to do this, you can just cut a piece of fabric a bit larger than the case top, lay it down, and fold the edges underneath. You'll want to iron out any creases and smooth the corners.

Plan the Contents of Each Case

In chapter 4 you made up a list of artifacts you thought would help illustrate the theme of this exhibition. You want to allow only the very best to make the final cut. Museum visitor studies specialists John Falk and Lynn Dierking wrote:

> It is critically important to be judicious in the number of ideas, objects, and experiences provided. Some museums present such a wealth of stimuli that visitors, especially children, may suffer from sensory overload. Children can become hyper-stimulated, running from one exhibit to the next, unable to focus their attention on any one thing for longer than a few seconds. (Falk and Dierking, 2013: 281)

Small museums have the unfortunate reputation of being dusty rooms crammed with stuff, like a disorganized antique store. Sadly, we have done much to deserve this. It is the natural desire of a collector to display the entire collection. But whether the object is butterflies or buttons, the visitors will only truly look at a few of them before their eyes glaze over.

Think of your artifact display as a stage set. Just show off the artifacts that illustrate your exhibition story.

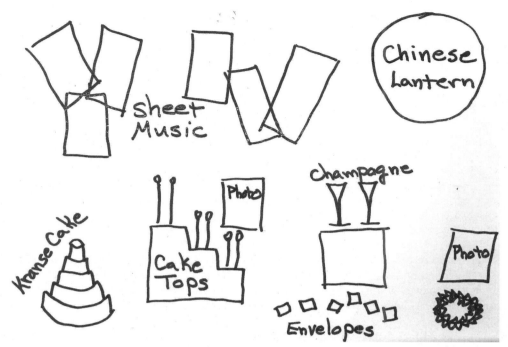

Image 7.73 Plan what you are going to put in each exhibit case. The best way is to make a sketch of what you would like to display. This will help you think about ways to get objects at different heights. This actual installation didn't come out exactly the same as the sketch, but it was helpful to have a plan. Hayward Area Historical Society, California.

Image 7.74 Actual installation based on the sketch. Hayward Area Historical Society, California.

Image 7.75 Think about creative ways to place objects in the case. Notice that the flat images and papers are on the side of the case. The guns are not mounted but are leaned against the case walls at interesting angles. Old Sturbridge Village, Massachusetts.

Risers and Stands

There are a few basic reasons for using risers and stands in exhibit cases:

- Place objects at various heights so they are visually interesting

- Tilt objects so they are easy to see and read

- Make special objects stand out

People can only comfortably move their heads 30 degrees from straight up. So to easily see objects in a case below their eye level, the objects need to be set up at angles. In addition, a person's field of vision is 30 degrees above and 40 degrees below eye level. Exhibit experts Craig and Phillip Thompson tell us that "where possible, [objects in] cases should be inclined at 30–45 degrees from the horizontal to provide better viewing for shorter patrons, children, and patrons using assistive devices" (Thompson and Thompson, 2014: 330). There is a drawing in the section on placing labels in cases that will be helpful as you arrange artifacts in cases.

Image 7.76 Even taller exhibit cases need to have flat artifacts tilted. Campaign buttons were stuck into fabric that was wrapped around a board and then tilted toward the visitor. The board was tilted by placing the back of it on a riser. The variety of heights of objects makes the exhibit more pleasant to view. Historical Society of Talbot County, Maryland.

Wood Risers

Cubes and rectangles made of wood are very versatile tools for organizing objects in an exhibit case. They allow you to raise heavy items as well as lightweight ones. Once again, they are relatively easy to construct and can be used over and over for decades. They are usually painted the same color as the interior of the case so that they are not distracting.

Wood risers are a little trickier to make than the cases because all six sides need to be enclosed. But they can be done by a volunteer with a little carpentry experience.

To make risers, you will need:

•   ½-inch plywood

•   Small wood blocks

•   Wood glue

•   Finish nails

Image 7.77 These heavy household utensils and equipment are displayed at different levels by the wood risers. Visitors can easily see each object. Notice that the labels are tilted for easy reading. In this exhibition, the sides of the cases are painted to match the walls, while the tops of the cases and the risers have all been painted white. Historical Society of Talbot County, Maryland.

These instructions are for a cube, but you can make the riser to any dimensions. You can even make the riser five sided and leave the bottom open.

- Cut plywood into six pieces.

- Cut blocks into twelve pieces, smaller than the sides of the cubes.

- Glue and nail the blocks onto the cut pieces as follows:
  - On two pieces, place blocks on four sides. Glue and nail.
  - On two pieces, place blocks on the top and bottom. Glue and nail.
  - Leave two pieces with no blocks.

- Glue the outside edges of each block.

- Put the pieces together as shown in the drawing.

- Set the nails and patch the holes if necessary.

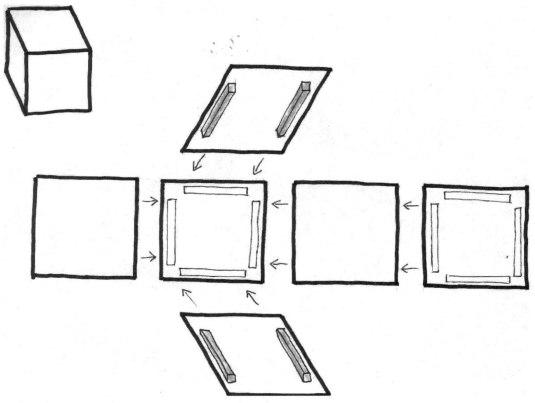

Image 7.78 Illustration of the construction of a wood tier.

Acrylic Risers

Acrylic risers and stands are available at most craft stores. They are usually clear, so they are practically invisible in the exhibit case. You can also find them online from a variety of vendors.

Inside the display case label:

BASEBALL, 1970

Baseball signed by the 1970 Campbell Little League team that placed second in the World Series.

Collection of the Campbell Historical Museum

SOFTBALL, 1987

Softball signed by the 1987 Quito Senior League team that won the World Series.

On Loan Courtesy of Jim Seeger

BASEBALL, 1976

Baseball signed by the 1976 Campbell Little League team that placed second in the World Series.

Collection of the Campbell Historical Museums
Donated by John Emery

Image 7.79 Acrylic stands come in all shapes and sizes. In this exhibit case, they were stacked up to create a variety of different heights, making the display more interesting than a line of balls. The label is being held up by an acrylic bookstand—you can barely see the supports at the bottom. Campbell Historical Museum, California. Photo by Shannon Dutra.

Mount Objects

Mounting the objects correctly is very important. You want to treat them very carefully so that they are safe while on exhibit. You can make do with materials at hand and still give your artifacts the best treatment possible.

Most artifacts will be in cases, but even there they need to be supported so they don't sag or break. You will want to provide stands, holders, or mounts. Museum experts Eugene Dillenburg and Janice Klein tell us:

> A wide variety of chemically inert plastic mounts, mini easels risers, and other display items are available commercially. Object mounts can also be made in-house using relatively inexpensive materials. Blocks of inert foam or wood, painted to match the cases or covered with appropriate fabric can be used to create multilevel platforms. . . . Monofilament (nylon fishing line, commonly sold in hardware stores) can be used to stabilize objects on their mounts while nails covered with inert plastic tubing can prevent objects from moving inside the case. (Dillenberg and Klein, 2012: 92)

More examples and photos are provided on our website.

Bent Wires and Metal

A basic way to mount items to the exhibit case is by using bent metal. You can create a base for the object, or just attach it the bottom of the exhibit case.

The wire or metal needs to be strong enough to hold the artifact and bendable enough to work with. Bend it into the shape and size needed to hold the object, and test it out before permanently

Image 7.80 A metal stand goes up the back of the artifact and wraps around to the front. Thinner wire can be used to hold the object and thicker, stronger wire for the stand. Flexible stands can be purchased from museum supply companies. Carver County Historical Society, Minnesota.

fastening it. Make sure it provides all the support the artifact needs, paying extra attention to delicate areas so it doesn't get damaged from being displayed. Flexible wire artifact stands can be purchased from museum supply companies, but in most cases you can make your own.

For objects made of a material that can be easily dented or scratched, it is best to cover the metal with a piece of flexible tubing. This is the type of tubing used for fish tank water pumps, and can be found at hardware or pet supply stores.

Acrylic Shapes, Stands, and Holders

Your local crafts store sells a great variety of plate holders, bookstands, and document holders. You can be creative in how you use them, and even turn them upside down or sideways to hold objects at just the right angle.

Cubes, rings, squares, rods, tubes, and any number of other shapes are available for purchase, online if not at your local store. Most of them are sold by the dozen at reasonable prices. These are invaluable for propping up objects.

Image 7.81 Stands were used in creative ways in this photo. The fan at left was displayed on a bookstand, although plate stands work even better. The bookstand supporting a book was turned upside down to get a lower angle. A sign holder, often used at restaurants to display the specials, was used to raise the end of a drop spindle off the surface and to hold it steady. The "vintage" flip phone is held on the acrylic stand with a little dab of putty to keep it from sliding off. Chemically inert putties called "Museum Wax" or "QuakeHOLD!" will keep objects firmly in place. It is also handy for preventing teacups from rattling on their saucers. Notice that the stand for the phone was used upside down to get the right angle.

Image 7.82 Acrylic cubes are perfect for holding a book open to a display a page. You want to support the book so there is no pressure on the spine. There are also specially made book cradles to hold a book open for display. Additionally, you can buy a roll of clear polyethylene book strap to hold the book open to the page you want. Historical Society of Talbot County, Maryland.

Image 7.83 Doll stands are useful for many objects other than dolls. They are made to go under a doll's arms to hold it upright. The wires can be bent into other shapes, and the height is adjustable. You will find them to be very versatile. The drop spindle at the right was tied to the stand with monofilament to keep it secure.

Objects Outside of Cases

Sometimes an artifact is mounted directly on the wall or floor. This is usually a larger, sturdier item than would be inside an exhibit case.

You must be certain that an object outside of a case is either mounted too high for visitors to reach or is behind a barrier. In general, if people can touch an object, they will. If visitors are allowed to touch the object, place a "please touch" sign near it to remove any doubts.

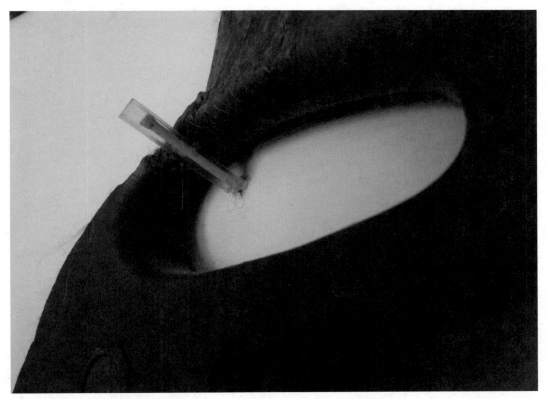

Image 7.84 You can see the clear plastic tubing over the nail holding this saw on the wall. The wood handle could be damaged by the bare metal screw, especially if it is left there for a long time. Fish tank air pump tubing works very well for this. Another nail holds the bottom of the saw so the weight is distributed.

Image 7.85 Bicycle hooks intended for use in a garage were perfect for mounting this rifle. The holders were padded and could be screwed into the wall. Be creative and wander around your hardware or home improvement store. You will find all sorts of useful items that you can use as they were not originally intended. Historical Society of Talbot County, Maryland.

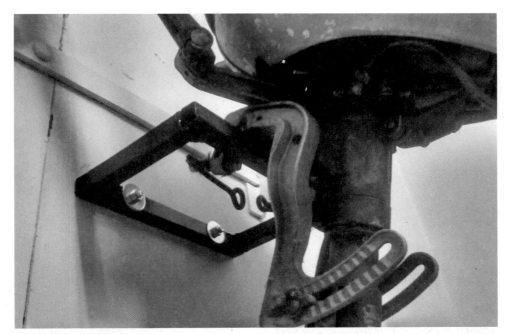

Image 7.86 A variety of outboard motors were displayed on this wall with metal mounts. In this case, they were extra secure because they were mounted into the solid wood shutters that are covering the window. Polk County Museum, Wisconsin.

Image 7.87 Pipe straps are among the most useful items you will find at a hardware store. In this exhibit, one was used to hold a bicycle wheel in place. It was even painted black and gray to match the wheel and the riser. The Cycling Museum of Minnesota exhibit at Hennepin History Museum, Minnesota.

Image 7.88 This letter was written on both sides, so a volunteer built this stand for it. A picture frame with glass on both sides works well for this type of paper artifact. The glass must be tight enough to hold the paper securely yet not so tight that it loosens the ink. This wooden stand placed on top of an exhibit case allows visitors to walk around and read both sides. Make sure to use UV-resistant glass for a project like this. Benson-Hammond House, Maryland.

Image 7.89 The original newspapers in this exhibit were encapsulated in acetate. The acetate was then mounted to the wall in the same way as a label. Hayward Area Historical Society, California.

To encapsulate a paper artifact, you will need:

- Acetate cut into two equal pieces, larger than the artifact

- Double-stick clear tape

Follow these simple steps:

- Measure the artifact and temporarily mark it on a piece of acetate.

- Place double-stick tape on the acetate, larger than the outline.

- Carefully place the artifact onto the acetate.

- Place the second piece of acetate on top.

- Press the pieces together.

- Trim the acetate to the outside edges of the tape, if desired.

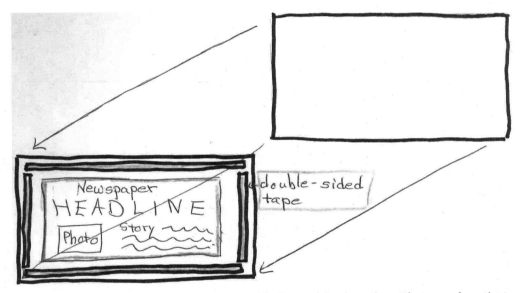

Image 7.90 Encapsulating paper items is easy to do. Be careful to keep the artifact away from the tape.

Lighting

Setting the lights will be the very last thing you do in your exhibition. You want every artifact, label, and panel in its final place before you aim the lights at them.

All of your labels need to be well lit. This goes for labels on the walls and labels in cases. You went to the trouble of writing great labels, so make sure your visitors can read them. It is very frustrating to visitors to be unable to identify an object because the label is in a dark corner.

You may remember from chapter 4 that lighting and color can be very important to the mood of your exhibition. Think of your exhibition space as a stage set—which items do you want to emphasize by shining a spotlight on them? "Since people are attracted to bright objects and areas of strong contrast in a room, one way to direct attention to an object is to focus more light on it than on its surrounding environment or background" (McLean, 1993: 142).

What parts of the room do you want to leave in shadows? "If, for example, there is an unsightly corner or a wall with thermostats and outlets on it, the entire area can be made to fall into shadow and practically disappear" (McLean, 1993: 143).

Your exhibition will bring visitors of all ages and physical abilities. As people age our eyes change, and we cannot see as well in dimly lit areas (Owsley, 2011: 1610). Make sure there is enough general lighting for everyone to be able to safely move around the room.

Setting your Lights

When your exhibition is completely installed, it is time to set the lights.

- Walk around the room and take note of where lights need to be aimed. Adjust your lights as needed.

- Go back around the room and see if the lights cause glare on any case vitrines or other shiny surfaces. Adjust your lights as needed.

- Walk around the room again and look slightly up to make sure there are no lights shining directly into your eyes. Remember that visitors may be taller or shorter than you are. "Position spot lights in such a way that they never shine directly into someone's eyes" (McLean, 1993: 143).

- One last time, check everything again and make sure you have lights where you need them.

Types of Lights

You already know that light will damage artifacts over time. Yet you need lighting in your exhibition. The good news is that new energy-efficient lights produce less damaging UV light and heat than older lights. Use a light meter to determine the amount of light on an object. There are light meter apps available for smartphones. Or you can probably find a photographer who still has one she or he can bring to the museum for a couple of hours.

Most types of lights will require a UV filter. There are UV filtering tubes designed for fluorescent tubes. You can buy UV filter film at a hardware store and use it for other lights.

The purchase of a track lighting system will be well worth the investment. You can buy a bit at a time just make sure you always get the exact same type with interchangeable lights. Track lights will allow you to adjust every light in the room.

If you only have overhead lights, you may want to use some clamp-on lights to provide highlights and lighten dark spots. When you are done positioning the lights, walk around the room and look at every object and panel using the checklist above.

Clamp-On Lights

Clamp-on lights provide a flexible way to set lighting on images and artifacts when you don't have track lighting. Even when you do have tracks, sometimes you need an extra spotlight on something.

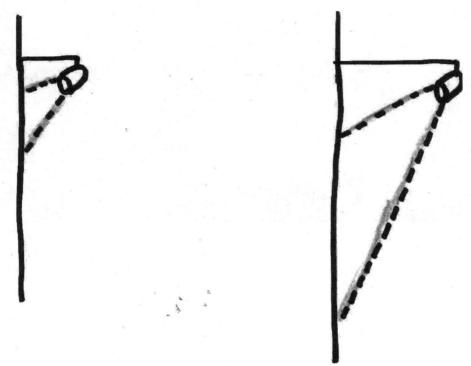

Image 7.91 Lights need to be away from the area they are lighting. As you can see, the same light fixture at the same angle provides light to a larger area when it is farther back. It also creates less glare. You will also get softer lighting. Adjust the clamp-on light for the farthest distance possible, or clamp it to something else farther away.

Track Lights

Make sure you get actual track lights where the lights can be moved anywhere along the track or even removed. This will allow you the most flexibility.

Place the tracks some distance from the wall. They should shine across to the object or label, not directly down on it. As with the clamp-on lamps, the fixture will light a larger area when it is farther back.

Image 7.92 Track lights outline the exhibition rooms in this museum. The lights can be slid along the track, allowing just about any place in the room to be lit. For a small room, this may be plenty of lights. For a larger room, getting light into the middle of the room could be difficult, requiring an additional track in the center. Hennepin History Museum, Minnesota.

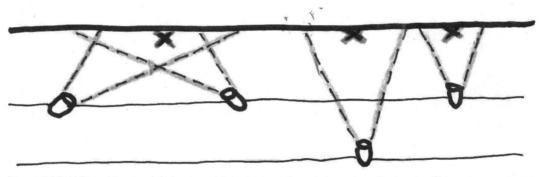

Image 7.93 When using track lights, consider which angle and distance will provide the best light with the least glare. You may want to use a track that is farther away—even on the other side of the room. Using two lights from the sides will help reduce glare.

Lights in Cases

If you are using exhibit cases that are tall or wide, it may be best to install a light inside the case itself. If you do this, keep in mind that you will need glass shelves to allow the light to reach objects and labels lower in the case. You will also want to arrange objects so that they are not in shadows cast by objects on higher shelves.

For tall cases, "puck" lights can be screwed or glued onto the inside of the top. You can purchase these small round lights at any hardware store. The best ones are LED lights, which are not only low energy but also low heat and low UV. You can even get battery-powered LED lights so you don't have to worry about where to plug it in. Just remember to keep extra batteries on hand.

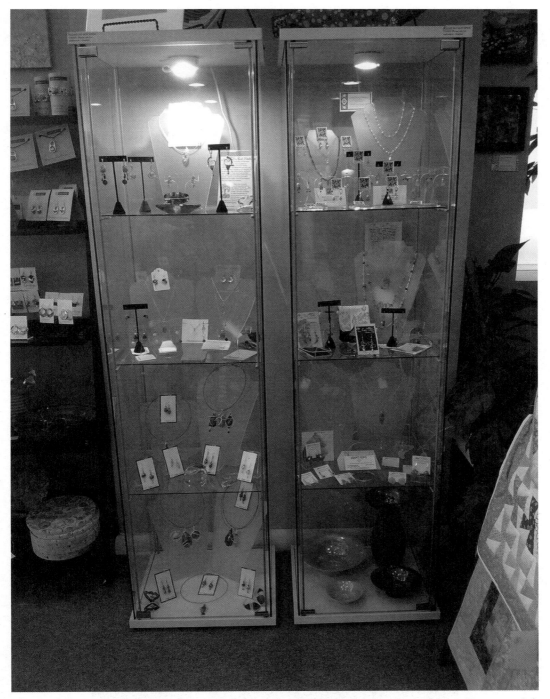

Image 7.94 These cases are in a retail store but work equally well in a museum exhibition. The one at left has an LED puck light, and the one at right has a standard puck light. The LED is much brighter. These cases are relatively inexpensive and are available at stores like Ikea. Green Phoenix store, Maryland.

Wide cases, such as those used in retail stores as jewelry counters, can benefit from an under-cabinet light. These are the lights sold to be put under kitchen cabinets. Again, the best lights at this time are LED lights because they have low energy use, heat, and UV.

Ceiling lights provide even lighting for people moving around the room, even if the cases are lit from within.

Both the lights in a case and the ceiling lights will need UV filters because flourescent lights can be damaging to artifacts. This problem can be addressed by slipping a UV filter tube over each lightbulb. The tubes can be reused when bulbs are replaced.

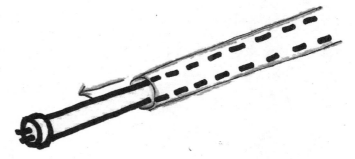

Image 7.95 UV filter tubes slide over fluorescent tubes and can be reused.

Reducing Daylight from Windows

If the room has natural light, you have two options: cover the windows with UV filters or cover the windows. As suggested by Heather Maximea, "It is usually recommended that these be completely boarded in, or at least blocked with removable panels. The latter approach can be effective in historic structures since it can respect the original architectural detailing" (Maximea, 2014: 77).

Image 7.96 You can see the edges of the UV film placed on the storm window inside the multipane window. The storm window provides insulation, and the UV film protects the artifacts on display in this historic house. Benson-Hammond House, Maryland.

Image 7.97 Internal shutters are used to cover the windows in this courthouse that is now used as a museum. Polk County History Museum, Wisconsin.

Lighting for Effect

Your exhibition space is like a stage set. You can use light and shadows to create emphasis on certain objects or labels.

Image 7.98 The hallway between exhibitions is a little darker than the exhibition spaces. This light on the introductory panel highlights it and draws the visitor into the exhibition. Interestingly, once you are in the exhibition, the panel no longer stands out because it is no lighter than any other panel or object. Hennepin History Museum, Minnesota.

Your exhibition is now complete. You and your team can put away all of your tools and equipment and get ready for the opening party. Be sure to take photos for your records, and send one to us at our website.

Sources

Blankenberg, Ngaire. "Virtual Experiences." In *Manual of Museum Exhibitions, Second Edition*. Edited by Barry Lord and Maria Piacente, 147–64. New York: Rowman & Littlefield, 2014.

DeMersman, Jim, in discussion with the author, 2001.

Dillenburg, Eugene, and Janice Klein. "Creating Exhibits: From Planning to Building." In *Small Museum Toolkit 5, Interpretation: Education, Programs, and Exhibits*. Edited by Cinnamon Catlin-Legutko and Stacy Klingler, 71–97. New York: Rowman & Littlefield, 2012.

Dutra, Shannon, personal communication with the author, 2016.

Falk, John H., and Lynn D. Dierking. *The Museum Experience Revisited*. Walnut Creek, CA: Left Coast Press, 2013.

Maximea, Heather. "Exhibition Facilities." In *Manual of Museum Exhibitions, Second Edition*. Edited by Barry Lord and Maria Piacente, 57–98. New York: Rowman & Littlefield, 2014.

McLean, Kathleen. *Planning for People in Museum Exhibitions*. Washington, DC: Association of Science-Technology Centers, 1993.

Neal, Arminta. *Help for the Small Museum, Second Edition*. Boulder, CO: Pruett Publishing, 1987.

Owsley, Cynthia. "Aging and Vision." *Vision Research* 51, no. 13 (July 1, 2011): 1610–22. http://www.sciencedirect.com/science/article/pii/S0042698910005110.

Science Buddies. "Science Fair Projects—Project Display Board Fonts." Accessed 2016. http://www.sciencebuddies.org/science-fair-projects/project_display_board_fonts.shtml.

Serrell, Beverly. *Exhibit Labels, An Interpretive Approach, Second Edition*. New York: Rowman & Littlefield, 2015.

Tang, Jacqueline. "Graphic Design." In *Manual of Museum Exhibitions, Second Edition*. Edited by Barry Lord and Maria Piacente, 314–21. New York: Rowman & Littlefield, 2014.

Thompson, Craig, and Philip Thompson. "Universal Design and Diversity." In *Manual of Museum Exhibitions, Second Edition*. Edited by Barry Lord and Maria Piacente, 322–34. New York: Rowman & Littlefield, 2014.

Uminowicz, Glen, in discussion with the author, 2004.

United States Department of Health and Human Services. "Anthropometric Reference Data for Children and Adults: United States, 2011–2014." *National Health Statistics Reports* (August 2016).

United States Department of Justice, Civil Rights Division. "Dimensions of Adult Sized Wheel-chairs." Accessed 2016. https://www.ada.gov/reg3a/figA3.htm.

United States Department of Justice, Civil Rights Division, "Maintaining Accessibility in Museums." 2009. Accessed 2016. http://www.ada.gov/business/museum_access.htm.

Wright, Lisa Dillon. "Curatorship and Content Development." In *Manual of Museum Exhibitions, Second Edition*. Edited by Barry Lord and Maria Piacente, 269–92. New York: Rowman & Littlefield, 2014.

Zuern, Erich. "Fabrication and Installation." In *Manual of Museum Exhibitions, Second Edition*. Edited by Barry Lord and Maria Piacente, 359–72. New York: Rowman & Littlefield, 2014.

Glossary

Accession: the process of logging a new artifact into the museum's collection.

Acid-free: paper products designed to be used in museum applications, which are made without acid. If paper is not marked "acid-free" you can assume that it is acidic.

ADA (Americans with Disabilities Act): an act of Congress that guaranteed equal opportunities and access for people with disabilities. Museums must provide access or "equivalent experiences" to all exhibitions.

Archival: materials made without chemicals that can off-gas or leach into artifacts.

Audience: members of the public who may be interested in an exhibition or public program.

Collection: the sum total of every artifact, document, and photo the museum owns.

Collections manager: the person who takes care of the objects in the museum's collection.

Conservation: keeping artifacts safe from harm now and in the future. Conservation intends to keep an artifact exactly as it is the day it was given to the museum.

Curator: the person who knows the content or subject matter of the exhibition.

Designer: the person who can carry out the intended look of the exhibit, and who knows how to arrange artifacts and labels to be attractive.

Educator: the person who makes sure the visitors understand the exhibit content and plans public programs.

Evaluation: the process of getting other people to let you know what they think of a concept or project.

Exhibit: an individual component in an exhibition, such as a single case or panel.

Exhibit furniture: permanent large items used to create an exhibition, such as exhibit cases and temporary walls.

Exhibition: an entire display of artifacts and images centered around a theme. All of the exhibits together create an exhibition.

Floor plan: a drawing of a room, possibly including furniture.

Font: the design of the letters used in creating written materials. Also called Typeface.

Formative evaluation: testing mock-up exhibits with audiences to see how they work.

Front-end evaluation: getting audience input into ideas for exhibition topics.

Grant: funds given to a nonprofit organization, usually for a specific project. Government agencies, private foundations, corporations, and individuals give grants.

Hands-on: exhibit components that visitors can touch and handle.

Installer: the person or people who physically put the exhibition together.

Interactive: exhibit components that visitors can use and manipulate, or that respond to visitor actions. This may be mechanical, such as flipping a switch, or electronic, such as a computer touch screen.

Interpretive label: a label that explains an artifact or image.

Label: the written text identifying an artifact or introducing a section of an exhibition.

Marketing: methods of letting the community know about the museum in general.

Mission: the statement of the museum's reason for being.

Model: a three-dimensional small version, intended to test the concept before making the full-sized item.

Monofilament: single-ply clear string. Fishing line is usually monofilament.

Off-gas: pollutants released from chemical mixtures as they evaporate in normal conditions. Also called VOC (volatile organic compounds).

Preparator: a museum professional who prepares objects for exhibit by making stands or holders for each one. This person will be trained in the weaknesses of each type of artifact material and in the inert qualities of stand materials.

Preservation: actions intended to keep an artifact intact for as long as possible. This may include some minor repairs.

Press release: a notice sent to newspapers, television, and radio stations and other news sources informing them of a specific event, such as an exhibition opening or a public program.

Program: an event open to the public, such as a lecture, demonstration, tour, or craft class.

Publicity: the methods of telling the community about specific exhibitions and programs.

Stanchion: a free-standing support post that is part of a barrier. It is the holder for a ribbon or rope that stretches between stanchions.

Summative evaluation: asking visitors what they think of a finished, installed exhibition.

Survey: a set of questions given to people with the purpose of finding out what they like or are interested in.

Target audience: the specific people who may be interested in an exhibition or public program, or who you want to be interested in it.

Typeface: the design of the letters used in creating written materials. Also called Font.

UV (ultraviolet) light: the portion of light that is beyond the range that humans can see but causes the most damage to artifacts. It is also the portion of light that causes sunburn.

Visitor studies: any type of survey or observation that gives a museum information about its visitors.

Vitrine: the clear plastic cube that makes up the top of an exhibit case.

VOC (volatile organic compounds): mixtures that can evaporate (or off-gas) in normal conditions and release pollutants.

Bibliography

American Society of Composers, Authors, and Publishers, "Using Copyrighted Music." Accessed June 2016. http://www.ascap.com/~/media/655449c494b748ba89edc4864655e1b6.pdf.

Blankenberg, Ngaire. "Virtual Experiences." In *Manual of Museum Exhibitions, Second Edition*. Edited by Barry Lord and Maria Piacente, 147–64. New York: Rowman & Littlefield, 2014.

Cognitive Sciences Stack Exchange. "Is It Better to Say 'Don't Forget' or 'Remember' in Written Encouragement?" Accessed 2016. http://cogsci.stackexchange.com/questions/7804/is-it -better-to-say-dont-forget-or-remember-in-written-encouragement.

DeMersman, Jim, in discussion with the author, 2001.

Dillenburg, Eugene, and Janice Klein. "Creating Exhibits: From Planning to Building." In *Small Museum Toolkit 5, Interpretation: Education, Programs, and Exhibits*. Edited by Cinnamon Catlin-Legutko and Stacy Klingler, 71–97. New York: Rowman & Littlefield, 2012.

Dutra, Shannon, personal communication with the author, 2016.

Falk, John H., and Lynn D. Dierking. *The Museum Experience Revisited*. Walnut Creek, CA: Left Coast Press, 2013.

Ferrara, Gabrielle. Unpublished paper for Exhibit Development course, University of Oklahoma, 2015.

Goforth, Teresa. "The Truth, the Whole Truth, and Nothing But the Truth: Researching Historical Exhibits." In *Small Museum Toolkit 5, Interpretation: Education, Programs, and Exhibits*. Edited by Cinnamon Catlin-Legutko and Stacy Klingler, 49–70. New York: Rowman & Littlefield, 2012.

Grewcock, Duncan. "Before, During, and After: Front-End, Formative, and Summative Evaluation." In *Manual of Museum Exhibitions, Second Edition*. Edited by Barry Lord and Maria Piacente, 33–39. New York: Rowman & Littlefield, 2014.

Hansen, Beth. Exhibit Development course materials, mock-up, University of Oklahoma, 2013.

Institute of Museum and Library Services. "Government Doubles Official Estimate: There Are 35,000 Active Museums in the U.S." IMLS.gov press release dated Monday, May 19, 2014.

Kamien, Janet. "An Advocate for Everything: Exploring Exhibit Development Models." *Curator* 44, no. 1 (2001): 114-28.

Kubier, Lauren. Unpublished paper for Exhibit Development course, University of Oklahoma, 2015.

Lord, Barry, and Maria Piacente. *Manual of Museum Exhibitions, Second Edition*. New York: Rowman & Littlefield, 2014.

Maximea, Heather. "Exhibition Facilities." In *Manual of Museum Exhibitions, Second Edition*. Edited by Barry Lord and Maria Piacente, 57-98. New York: Rowman & Littlefield, 2014.

McLean, Kathleen. *Planning for People in Museum Exhibitions*. Washington, DC: Association of Science-Technology Centers, 1993.

Moeller, Tamerra P. "Sensory Changes in Older Adults: Implications for Museums." Museum Education *Roundtable Reports* 9, no. 4 (Fall 1984): 6-8.

National Park Service. *Museum Handbook, Part I Museum Collections*. National Park Service, 2016.

Neal, Arminta. *Help for the Small Museum, Second Edition*. Boulder, CO: Pruett Publishing, 1987.

Owsley, Cynthia. "Aging and Vision." *Vision Research* 51, no. 13 (July 1, 2011): 1610-22. http://www.sciencedirect.com/science/article/pii/S0042698910005110.

Science Buddies. "Science Fair Projects—Project Display Board Fonts." Accessed 2016. http://www.sciencebuddies.org/science-fair-projects/project_display_board_fonts.shtml.

Screven, C. G. "Exhibitions and Information Centers: Some Principles and Approaches." *Curator* 29, no. 2 (1986): 109-37.

Serrell, Beverly. *Making Exhibit Labels: A Step-by-Step Guide*. Nashville, TN: American Association for State and Local History, 1983.

Serrell, Beverly. *Exhibit Labels, An Interpretive Approach, Second Edition*. New York: Rowman & Littlefield, 2015.

Smithsonian Institution. "The Making of Exhibitions: Purpose, Structure, Roles and Process." Washington, DC: Smithsonian Institution, Office of Policy and Analysis, 2002.

Soren, Barbara, and Jackie Armstrong. "Qualitative and Quantitation Audience Research." In *Manual of Museum Exhibitions, Second Edition*. Edited by Barry Lord and Maria Piacente, 40-54. New York: Rowman & Littlefield, 2014.

Tang, Jacqueline. "Graphic Design." In *Manual of Museum Exhibitions, Second Edition*. Edited by Barry Lord and Maria Piacente, 314-21. New York: Rowman & Littlefield, 2014.

Thompson, Craig, and Philip Thompson. "Universal Design and Diversity." In *Manual of Museum Exhibitions, Second Edition*. Edited by Barry Lord and Maria Piacente, 322–34. New York: Rowman & Littlefield, 2014.

Uminowicz, Glen, in discussion with the author, 2004.

United States *Department of Health and Human Services.* "Anthropometric Reference Data for Children and Adults: United States, 2011–2014." *National Health Statistics Reports (August 2016).*

United States Department of Justice, Civil Rights Division. "Dimensions of Adult-Sized Wheelchairs." Accessed 2016. https://www.ada.gov/reg3a/figA3.htm.

United States Department of Justice, Civil Rights Division. "Maintaining Accessibility in Museums." 2009. Accessed 2016. http://www.ada.gov/business/museum_access.htm.

Wilson, Michelle S. Unpublished paper for Exhibit Development course, University of Oklahoma, 2015.

Wright, Lisa Dillon. "Curatorship and Content Development." In *Manual of Museum Exhibitions, Second Edition*. Edited by Barry Lord and Maria Piacente, 269–92. New York: Rowman & Littlefield, 2014.

Zuern, Erich. "Fabrication and Installation." In *Manual of Museum Exhibitions, Second Edition*. Edited by Barry Lord and Maria Piacente, 359–72. New York: Rowman & Littlefield, 2014.

Index

layout. *See* floorplan
light: arrangement, 29, 34, 127, 151–58; dramatic,
   153–55, 157–58; glare, 48, 69, 123, 152, 153,
   154; in cases, 88, 92, 154–56; room, 47, 48, 68,
   152–57; uv (ultraviolet) light. *See* preservation

mannequin,94, 100–5
map strip. *See* hanging
marketing, 8, 10, 55
mission, 1, 2, 3, 21, 51
mock-up, 55–65, 111, 136
model: of exhibit. *See* mock-up; of floorplan, 33,
   34–36
mood. *See* appearance
mount. *See* objects—mount; *See* label—mount.

objects, 1, 16–7, 23–28, 37–38, 41–42, 43, 54, 106;
   display of, 10, 24–25, 82, 87, 88, 93, 94, 119,
   122, 124, 136–51; mount, 136, 139, 144–46. *See
   also* photos.

paint, 10, 29, 36, 67, 69–70, 74, 78, 82, 83, 90, 94,
   100, 125, 136, 140, 141, 144, 149
panel. *See* wall panel
period rooms, 93, 98–100
permanent exhibit, 2–4
photos, 23, 24, 26–27, 37–38, 44, 85, 110, 120;
   display of, 10, 69, 73, 76, 110, 116–18, 131–33,
   136. *See also* objects
picture rail. *See* hanging
preparator. *See* volunteers
preservation: acid-free, 117, 118; during exhibition,
   24–26, 136; humidity, 25, 26, 136; off-gas, 83,
   100, 104, 105; temperature, 25; uv (ultraviolet)
   light, 25–26, 110, 116, 136, 152, 156–57; voc
   (volatile organic compounds), 69, 83
programs, public, 8, 10, 19–20
publicity. *See* marketing

risers. *See* exhibit furniture
room layout. *See* floorplan

section heading. *See* label
signs. *See* label

staff. *See* volunteers
stanchion. *See* barrier
story, 13–22, 33, 42–43. *See also* topic
summative evaluation. *See* evaluation
survey. *See* evaluation

target audience. *See* audience
temporary exhibit, 2–3, 16, 18, 70, 92. *See also*
   exhibit furniture–temporary walls
theater, 51, 68, 94, 100
timeline, 10–11
title. *See* label
topic, 3, 4, 13–22, 24, 28–29, 37–38, 43, 50, 54, 92;
   object based, 16; phenomenon demonstration,
   17; people based, 17–18; and room appearance,
   29; topic based, 17. *See also* story
typeface. *See* font.

UV (ultraviolet) light. *See* preservation

video, 31, 51, 114–15
visitors. *See* audience
visitor studies. *See* evaluation
vitrine. *See* exhibit furniture
VOC (volatile organic compounds). *See*
   preservation
volatile organic compounds (VOC). *See*
   preservation
volunteers, 7–12, 15, 42, 51, 54, 55, 70, 128, 135;
   collections manager, 8–10, 23–27; curator,
   7–10, 16, 19, 23–27, 41–48, 55–65; designer,
   7–10, 29–30, 55–65; educator, 7–10, 19–21,
   41–48, 55–65; installer, 8–10, 29–36, 55–65,
   67, 70, 80, 83, 93, 94, 110, 131, 135, 140,
   150; marketing, 8–10; museum store, 8–10,
   50; project manager, 8–10; preparator, 136;
   receptionist, 31, 109, 113, 114; recruiting, 8, 15,
   20, 51, 68, 70; roles, 7–11

wall, 31–35, 69, 73–74, 75, 121; paint, 10, 29, 36,
   69–70; permanent, 69–70, 73–75; temporary,
   78–81, 100
wall panel, 75, 131–36
website. *See* auxiliary materials

About the Author

Beth Hansen started her twenty-plus-year museum career through a graduate program, but she has always worked at very small museums where she was the entire exhibit development/construction staff. Her mix of academic training and practical experience led her to teach workshops on creating exhibits for other small museums. Over the years she has been lucky enough to work with creative volunteers and ingenious museum directors who have come up with great ideas for do-it-ourselves projects.

She developed and teaches the Exhibit Development class for the Museum Studies graduate program at the University of Oklahoma. As a faculty member, she has access to the latest research in visitor studies. Sharing this information with volunteers at small museums is her goal for *Great Exhibits!*